AF339084

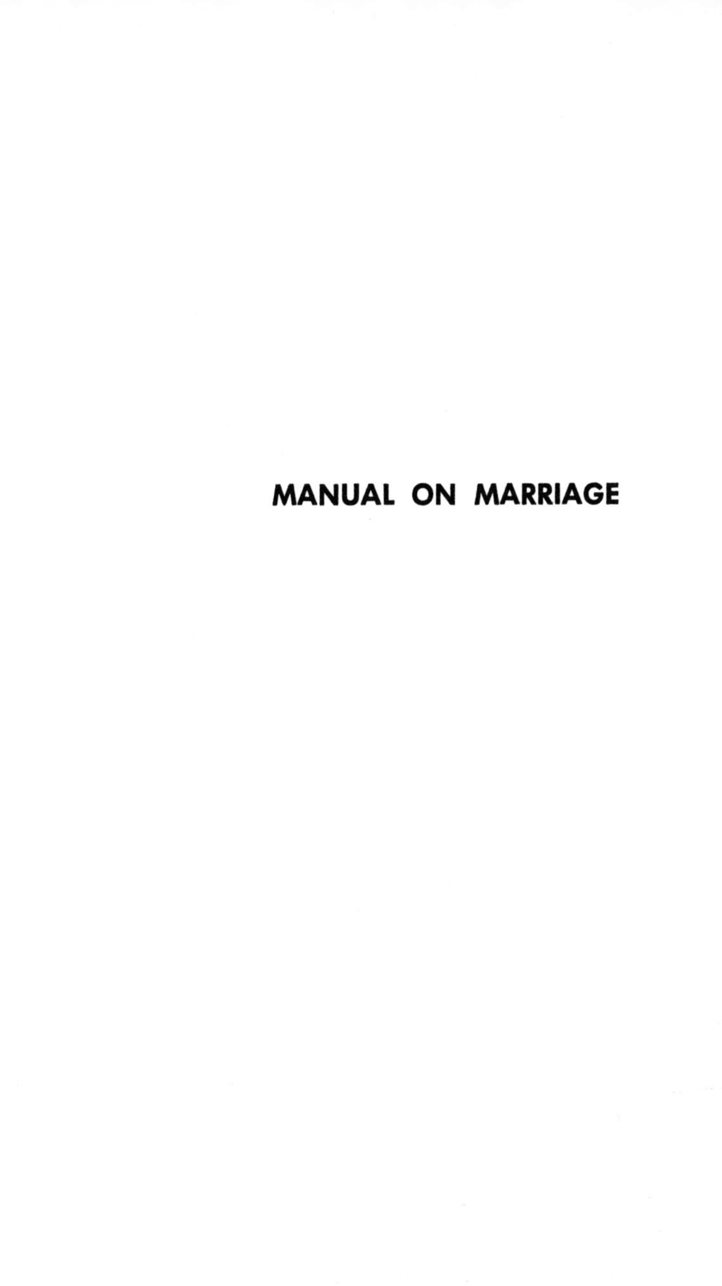

MANUAL ON MARRIAGE

Reorganized
CHURCH OF JESUS CHRIST
of Latter Day Saints

Manual on Marriage

Edited by the
Worship Committee

1971
HERALD HOUSE
Independence, Missouri

Copyright © 1971
HERALD PUBLISHING HOUSE
Independence, Missouri

All rights in this book are reserved. No part of the text may be reproduced in any form without written permission of the publishers, except brief quotations used in connection with reviews in magazines or newspapers.

Library of Congress Catalog
Card Number: 79-162861
ISBN 0-8309-0049-7

Printed in U.S.A.

FOREWORD

This Manual on Marriage has been written to assist priests and elders in counseling persons who are preparing for marriage. The manual was brought together by members of the Council of Twelve Apostles who were serving as a Worship Committee under assignment of the First Presidency.

We acknowledge with deep gratitude the help of experienced ministers, Dr. Roy A. Cheville and Franklyn S. Weddle. We have included a modified chapter of *Sacraments and Ordinances of the Church,* by Alfred Yale and Charles Brockway (Herald House, 1962).

Your attention is called to the section "Planning Your Wedding Service" which is also printed separately for those who contemplate marriage.

We hope that the sacramental significance of marriage will be enhanced by use of this book.

THE DIVISION OF PROGRAM SERVICES

Reed M. Holmes

CONTENTS

THE MARRIAGE CEREMONY CIVIL AND RELIGIOUS

Christian marriage is sacramental in nature.[1] When approached through the church, it becomes a sacrament in every sense.

1. Marriage is commanded by God.
2. Its covenant is given before God.
3. It is administered by priesthood.
4. Its symbol is the joining of hands.
5. Its sacrifice is the joining of two lives as one.
6. It is a public ceremony.
7. There are prescribed words given.

If any part is left out it becomes only a ceremony, possibly religious in nature but less sacramental.

We should note that God, not man, instituted the marriage covenant. "And I, the Lord God, said unto mine Only Begotten, that it was not good that the man should be alone; wherefore, I will make an help meet for him."[2]

"Therefore shall a man leave his father and his mother, and shall cleave unto his wife; and they shall be one flesh."[3]

"I say unto you, that whoso forbiddeth to marry, is not ordained of God, for marriage is ordained of God unto man; wherefore it is lawful that he should have one wife, and they twain shall be one flesh."[4]

Exact words are given which must be used in the ceremony of uniting two in marriage:

"You both mutually agree to be each other's companion, husband and wife, observing the legal rights belonging to this condition; that is, keeping yourselves wholly for each other, and from all others, during your lives?"[5]

And to this ceremony the words of benediction are given:

"May God add his blessings and keep you to fulfill your covenants from henceforth and for ever. Amen."[6]

The marriage ceremony is not necessarily a religious event since it is under the regulation of the government and may be performed by those who are authorized by the state. In some nations a civil ceremony is required regardless of any religious service the couple may choose to have. In other countries the minister may act for both church and state. All Christian couples should be urged to expand their marriage covenant beyond any civil requirement. They should be encouraged to enter this holy estate with a deep sense of its sacramental nature. In those countries where a separate civil ceremony is required, the religious ordinance should also be observed, wherever permissible. While marriages are authorized by governments and may be made legal by civil ceremonies, the religious aspect of marriage requires recognition of God through the church.[7]

THE PURPOSE OF MARRIAGE

The primary function of marriage is the perpetuation of the race. The following scriptures touch on this point:

"And I, God, blessed them, and said unto them, Be fruitful, and multiply, and replenish the earth, and subdue it."[8]

This statement made to our first parents was repeated to Noah and his family after the earth had been depopulated by the flood:

"And a commandment I give unto you, Be ye fruitful and multiply; bring forth abundantly on the earth, and multiply therein."[9]

A similar statement was given to the church in these latter days: "Marriage is ordained of God unto man; wherefore it is lawful that he should have one wife, and they twain shall be one flesh, and all this that the earth might answer the end of its creation; and that it might be filled with the measure of man, according to his creation before the world was made."[10]

But the procreative function is expressed in a relationship based on the marriage covenant so that the children conceived may be raised to maturity in an atmosphere conducive to their proper training and care. Obviously, children may be begotten outside of marriage, but the Christian family relationship is the stabilizing force in the child's environment by which the qualities of love and other spiritual graces can be invested in his personality.

There is a further and equally important purpose of the marriage covenant—companionship. "And I, the Lord God, said unto mine Only Begotten, that it was not good that the man should be alone."[11] Man and woman become husband and wife in mutual dependence and affection, growing together toward God.

The establishment of a satisfactory marriage relationship involves elements of self-surrender. As a matter of common experience, everyone who makes the covenant needs to learn to surrender his own will to that of the marriage partner at times. He needs to appreciate that he is not free to choose always as he wishes. He must now consider the wishes or needs of the other person. He must realize that firmly established personal habits must be modified so that harmonious relations can be carried out.

Jesus said, "Whosoever will lose his life in this world, for my sake, shall find it in the world to come."[12] This principle can be applied to marriage. In the subordination of self to the marriage union, we learn something of what it means to subordinate self to the will of God. By learning self-surrender in marriage, we are better able to surrender self in other ways.

The experiences of bringing forth and caring for children call for further subordination of self-interest. As children grow, parents learn to feel for them in somewhat the same manner Christ feels for all of us. Children sometimes suffer as a result of their actions. When they are hurt, loving parents suffer with them. Part of the anguish arises from the fact that parents sometimes can see in advance the result of their children's unwise choices and yet know that they cannot compel their children to choose a wiser course. Parents lose sleep and shed tears over children as they make choices which tend to lead them away from God. Yet children must be given the freedom to make more and more choices of their own as they grow into maturity.

One young man, reared in a devout church family, told his father that he was old enough now to make up his own mind. He had determined that he would not attend church anymore because he had all of the church he wanted. His father's reply was, "You are right. You are old enough to make up your own mind about these things. But there are two things you can't keep me from doing. One of them is loving you. The other is praying for you."

As parents and children have many and varied experiences together, we may learn to appreciate the deep concern which Christ exercises for his children. We can begin to understand what it meant for him to weep over Jerusalem. We can comprehend what it meant for him to suffer when his people rejected him. We may comprehend the joy of the Lord when parents and children live through painful experiences out of which comes deeper mutual understanding. This deeper insight brings us closer to God and helps us to understand more and more about our relationships with God.

MAINTAINING THE COVENANT

The word of God first emphasizes the affirmative obligations of the marriage covenant: "Thou shalt love thy wife with all thy heart, and shall cleave unto her and none else." But the obligations also require a strict personal discipline. "He that looketh upon a woman to lust after her, shall deny the faith, and shall not have the Spirit; and if he repents not, he shall be cast out."[13]

"Verily I say unto you, that whatever persons among you having put away their companions for the cause of fornication, ... ye shall not cast them out from among you; but if ye shall find that any persons have left their companions for the sake of adultery, and they themselves are the offenders, and their companions are living, they shall be cast out from among you. And again I say unto you, that ye shall be watchful and careful, with all inquiry, that ye receive none such among you if they are married, and if they are not married, they shall repent of all their sins, or ye shall not receive them."[14]

"Have ye not read, that he who made man at the beginning, made him, male and female, and said, For this cause shall a man leave father and mother, and shall cleave to his wife; and they twain shall be one flesh? Wherefore they are no more twain, but one flesh.

What, therefore, God hath joined together, let no man put asunder. . . . Whosoever shall put away his wife, except for fornication, and shall marry another, committeth adultery; and whoso marrieth her that is put away, doth commit adultery."[15]

In these days of easy divorce it is important to reexamine the divinely established purposes of marriage. Marriage must be interpreted as a covenant which is a sacred vow. God is concerned that the values of human life should be enhanced and fulfilled in terms of the marriage covenant.

THE STANDARDS AND PROCEDURES OF MARRIAGE

On August 17, 1835, a general assembly of the church unanimously adopted a resolution setting forth the church's procedure for wedding ceremonies. This now appears in Section 111 of the Doctrine and Covenants. It offers guidance concerning such matters as the public interest, appropriate setting, and the authority by which marriages are solemnized in the church.

MARRIAGE IS A PUBLIC CONCERN

"We believe, that all marriages in this Church of Christ of Latter Day Saints should be solemnized in a public meeting."[16]

". . . not done covertly or clandestinely. Even though it be a 'private home wedding,' it is in a sense 'public' in that it is not secret but is known to the neighborhood."[17]

Society has a stake in every marriage and has a perfect right to take cognizance of marriages and to legislate to govern them in ways beneficent to society, since the family thus established is an integral part of society; and further because the well-being of the offspring of the union is a matter of public concern.

THE MARRIAGE CEREMONY IN THE HOME

Since marriage is ordained of God, and when properly entered into and practiced brings us closer to him, the wedding should be essentially a religious ceremony. It ought to be performed by priestly authority in the church. Moreover, it, like other ceremonial ordinances, is best performed in a public place of worship. The wording of Section 111:1 provides that marriages performed by other authorities and in other places are recognized as valid. This recognition, however, refers not to the sacramental qualities but to the laws of the land.

If for some reason it is not practical to have a public ceremony in a house of worship, then the next choice is to have it performed in a chapel, in the home of the minister, or in the home of one of the participants. It should be entered into with adequate preparation—not a hasty ceremony. There is rightful concern over any marriage wherein the first contact with the minister is on the same day, and sometimes at the same hour the ceremony is supposed to occur. Such arrangements should be discouraged.[18]

While the legality of marriages performed under non-ecclesiastical circumstances is not challenged, a wedding performed under any conditions which make the ceremony into an exhibition or publicity stunt is not in keeping with the purpose and spirit of Christian marriage. Ministers of the church are urged to refrain from officiating in such ceremonies.

MARRIAGE WITHIN THE CHURCH

"We believe that it is not right to prohibit members of this church from marrying out of the church, if it be their determination so to do, but such persons will be considered weak in the faith of our Lord and Savior Jesus Christ."[19]

This passage is best understood against the background of the situation of the church in 1835. There was severe persecution in the Kirtland area. The first "exposé" of Mormonism was written and published by Mr. Howe, editor of the Painesville *Telegraph*, whose bitter opposition to the church was inflamed in spite of, or perhaps as a consequence of, his wife becoming a member. There was good reason to fear the outcome of religious conflicts in the home. Feeling ran high among members of differing denominations. Under such circumstances as these, domestic conflict over religion was a serious problem. Perhaps the basic issues to which this instruction is addressed have not been adequately solved even yet, though they have taken on dimensions which may justify a different term in defining today the problems of interfaith marriages.

This passage was not intended to prohibit such marriages, however, and should not be so interpreted. The great variety of circumstances make it unreasonable and unjust to apply a blanket rule as though it were equally valid for every situation. Under some circumstances the choice may lie between marrying "out of the church" or remaining unmarried. But those who cross religious lines in marriage should do so thoughtfully and in an awareness of the potential problems.

It is the responsibility of parents and church leaders to see to it that young people have reasonable opportunity to meet a variety of other church young people. Such opportunities are provided in district and regional gatherings, youth camps, Graceland College, and other group activities and events which provide for intermingling of young people of mutual faith. These gatherings are not marriage bureaus, but they do provide opportunity for wholesome fellowship among the young people who share religious convictions at a time when they are choosing their life partners.

It is true that interfaith marriage decreases the chances of either husband or wife church member remaining in the faith. A study by the Department of Statistics shows that both Latter Day Saint men and women have the best opportunity for significant and active church life if they are married to Latter Day Saint companions.

This problem is not unique to our faith. It is shared by all churches. The committee on marriage and the home, appointed by the Federal Council of Churches of Christ in America, in its report of March 1932 stated:

"Wherever human wedlock is regarded as possessing a sacred character and denotes a conjunction of souls and minds as well as physical union, it becomes apparent that harmony in their religious sentiments is of first importance to those united in marriage. . . .

"Not only for the sake of their own happiness but also for social reasons, for the sake of the stability of the new family created by their union, it is greatly to be desired that there should be agreement in religious faith on the part of those who marry, and it is essential that there should be mutual respect and forbearance. . . .

"It is evident that the problem of mixed marriages is not simple, and that it is not susceptible of easy solution. Religion is a basic interest in human life, and differences in religion, if these are fundamental, are aggravated by ecclesiastical interference. . . .

"Statistics bearing upon the matter are not adequate, but there is reason to suppose that marriages of this sort are highly unstable; furthermore, that in very many cases they lead either to the departure of both parents from the practices of religion or at least to the abandonment of any attempt on their part to provide for the religious education of their children."

Let it be noted that marriage in the church is no guarantee alone of a happy marriage. Common understanding about religion and sharing of spiritual ideals is an important factor making for stability of the home, but it is only one factor. Other factors include common interests and friends, common social background, common mature comprehension of the principles of finance in the home.

It should be further recognized that marriage in the church does not exempt either party from the usual and necessary adjustments required to make the marriage successful. Marriage is not so much a matter of *finding* the right partner as *being* the right partner. Each partner must undergo self-surrender for the sake of the new union. A common covenant with God by way of baptism, and mutual endeavor to live up to the terms of this covenant should help considerably in adjusting to married life. There is no substitute in marriage for the ideals promulgated by the church. All marriages of members of the church should be enriched by gospel ministries which encourage them to the fullest possible measure of spiritual oneness.

Elbert A. Smith once stated, "A sacrament involves a sacred covenant either explicitly stated or tacitly accepted." It seems possible that marriages of church members not originally fully entered in harmony with spiritual requirements may yet attain sacramental conditions through tacit acceptance of and abiding in the standards of Latter Day Saint marriage and home life.

Let us summarize:

1. Other things being equal, the chances of both having a happy marriage and of continued growth spiritually are improved by marriage in the church.

2. Entering into marriage is a significant event. We can expect help and direction by constant prayer.

3. All young church members should seek wide fellowship among other church youth.

4. Marriage within the church is of itself no guarantee of a happy union. Other factors which make for a stable

marriage must also be considered.

5. The nonmember whom the church member proposes to marry should understand how the member feels about his church prior to marriage.

6. The church member should endeavor to win his nonmember partner to the faith prior to marriage rather than hoping that marriage will tend to bring him into the fellowship. This is best done by demonstration of what his faith means to him and requires the exercise of patience, persistence, and selfless love.

"FOR EACH OTHER AND FROM ALL OTHERS"

The key clause of the marriage contract is "For each other and from all others." It has both positive and negative aspects. It is not sufficient to stress the negative feature of the contract. While it is true that the contract is violated if one of the partners commits adultery, it is broken also if one of the partners fails to keep himself *for* the other. A man who squanders the family income in ways detrimental to his wife and children violates the clause "keeping yourselves wholly for each other." A wife who grossly neglects her household duties to the detriment of her family does likewise. It is possible to adulterate the marriage covenant with such excesses of intoxicants, gambling, or any other type of self-interest that the covenant is eroded and even destroyed. Sometimes husbands or wives become so involved in their vocations that they violate the spirit of the marriage covenant.

The constructive aspect of the marriage covenant requires both parties to give their best intelligence and mature understanding to the problem of happy, mutual adjustment.

If one partner has grossly violated the marriage covenant this may lead to conditions for which no solution is found except divorce. It should be understood, however, that each situation has its own particular circumstances. Even when the contract is violated in either the positive or negative aspects, it is not required that the other partner seek a divorce. The first response of the innocent spouse should be an effort in the spirit of forgiveness and compassion to reestablish that which was lost.

WHAT GOD HAS JOINED TOGETHER

"What God hath joined together, let no man put asunder." This phrase does not appear in the basic wedding ceremony for Latter Day Saints. It is widely used, however, and immediately leads to another question: Who has God joined together? Surely this does not necessarily include all who share in a marriage ceremony. Even the civil law requires integrity and forthright mutual commitment. Fraud and certain kinds of misrepresentation are grounds for annulment in many legal jurisdictions. Just as the act of going down into the water and coming forth again does not constitute baptism unless accompanied by an inner spiritual change, so also the act of being united in a ceremony of marriage does not initiate a spiritual union unless the spiritual elements which should accompany it are present. Marital experience is initiated by the wedding ceremony but it is accompanied by mutual affection, and Christian marriage leads to a growing together and a oneness which ought not to be dissolved.

"In these days of hasty and thoughtless marriages, many people who live together cannot conceivably have been joined together by God. A large proportion of such 'marriages' are recognized by the courts to be not marriages at all, and are annulled. Others, which are legally binding, have never carried the sanction of Divinity. Consider, for a moment, the large number of hasty and disastrous war weddings entered into in an atmosphere of personal and patriotic emotion shot through by fear. Consider again the case of clean and splendid women married and thereby immediately infected with a disease the existence of which they were previously only technically aware. Consider again, the large number of people married for considerations of wealth, position, and safety. God is willing to join together even those persons who marry under these conditions if, recognizing their situation, they join him in strengthening the bonds that unite them and in creating still other bonds. But here is the point: these bonds ought to be created before the marriage ceremony is performed; and persons who embark upon a marital career without such bonds of union between them are not joined by God and run grave risk that they never will be.

"Marriage is a spiritual enterprise which can only be made effective by truly Christian people. For others it may be a physical and legal union blessed by mutual affection of the highest possible order, but unless it has the spiritual quality which is achieved by persons who live in the light of Christ, it lacks the full measure of divine sanction and lacks also something of the stability and permanence which was contemplated in its institution."[20]

INSTRUCTIONS TO THE PRIESTHOOD

Since the rite of marriage is sacred in the sight of God, a grave responsibility is laid on the priesthood, especially on the officiating minister, to give premarital instruction and to properly administer the rite of marriage. The success or failure of marriage largely depends upon how well the contracting parties have been prepared for this holy estate. It becomes necessary, therefore, for the minister to set forth in simple, understandable terms some of the requirements and the instructions which will help make this event blessed in the sight of God. It may be helpful for him to review the following principles and procedures before solemnizing a marriage:

1. The presiding elder is the chief administrative officer of the congregation. All weddings should be conducted with the consent of the presiding elder even though some other elder or priest is to officiate.

2. The minister should arrange counseling sessions with the couple in harmony with the recommendations and information supplied by Dr. Roy A. Cheville in a later section of this manual.

3. The minister shall solemnize a marriage only if the contracting parties have given him sufficient time for these arrangements and counseling prior to the date set for the marriage. He shall ascertain the right of the parties, according to the laws both of the land and the church, to contract a marriage. If there has been a previous marriage, a complete inquiry shall be made by the minister. Where a divorce has been involved, sufficient time will be required for the necessary research through the proper church channels before there is an authorization of this marriage.[21]

4. The minister shall conform to the laws of the government which authorizes the marriage as well as to the laws of the church. It is essential that every minister who is to perform marriages acquaint himself with the civil laws governing them and assure himself of his authority to officiate.

5. Since it is obvious that only a limited amount of instruction can be given and assimilated in a few days, the minister should prepare for these periods of instruction with considerable care so that he will be as thorough as possible in his ministry.

6. The minister shall make the following records and reports:

    a. Fill in all information, sign, and obtain signatures as required on the marriage certificate of the state or country. These signatures shall be obtained immediately following the ceremony or as otherwise required by the laws of the state or country.

b. See that a proper report of this marriage is sent to the Department of Statistics.

c. The minister should keep a personal record of all marriages solemnized by him. The laws of nations, states, and provinces require such a record to be kept. This is true concerning marriages which take place outside the auspices of the church which involve nonmembers as well as members of the church.

---

1. "Marriage should be entered into soberly, worthily, and after mature consideration. Members of the church should marry only such persons as realize the sacramental nature of the marriage covenant and are willing to abide by its necessary conditions as well as to enjoy its rewards."—General Conference Resolution 1034, par. 4, *Rules and Resolutions*, Herald House, Independence, Mo., 1964, p. 180.
2. Gen. 2:23, 24.
3. Gen. 2:30.
4. D. and C. 49:3a-b.
5. D. and C. 111:2b.
6. D. and C. 111:2d.
7. "God is concerned in every marriage. Marriages should therefore be solemnized with dignity in a setting conducive to worship. To this end, simplicity, propriety, and frugality in the

service and its appointments are advised. Civil marriages, though legally acceptable, recognize only the civil significance of the compact and so tend to minimize the spiritual values involved. In order to preserve the sacramental nature of marriage in countries where civil marriages are required by law, a second ceremony is encouraged. This ceremony is to be conducted by authorized priesthood in the recommended worshipful setting."—G.C.R. 1034, par. 5.

8. Gen. 1:30.
9. Gen. 9:14.
10. D. and C. 49:3.
11. Gen. 2:23.
12. Matt. 16:28.
13. D. and C. 42:7d.
14. D. and C. 42:20.
15. Matt. 19:4-6, 9.
16. D. and C. 111:1b.
17. Elbert A. Smith, *Marriage and Home Building.*
18. "Members of the Melchisedec priesthood or priests of the Aaronic order may solemnize marriages when so permitted by civil law (Doctrine and Covenants 111:1b, c). Officiating ministers should require that they be given sufficient time by the parties seeking their services to enable them to make such investigation and to give such instruction and counsel as they deem helpful in maintaining the sacramental nature of the marriage covenant and of the marriage itself."—G.C.R. 1034, par. 6.
19. D. and C. 111:1d.
20. F. Henry Edwards, *Fundamentals,* Herald House, 1960, Independence, Mo.: pp. 270, 271.
21. General Conference Resolution 1034, par. 9.

COUNSELING ON FAMILY LIVING

Pre-Marriage Interviewing
in
Our Inclusive Program
on
Family Living

Roy A. Cheville

PREFACE

This chapter approaches the overall field of family living and indicates some significant areas of counseling. The reader will note that it is suggested that the areas of concern herein expressed can be best approached when included in the total ministry which should be given through the years. We should consciously strive to achieve this ideal.

This chapter also recognizes that some will come for marriage who have not been prepared by this long-range ministry. When this is true the responsible minister, or ministers, must do all possible to share in such counseling prior to marriage. In many instances this counseling should continue after marriage.

The following material is presented as a guide to help you in this important area of your ministry.

PRE-MARRIAGE INTERVIEWING

Marriage counseling is urgently needed today. The field is so complex that the honest man may be inclined to say, "This is too much for me." But any ministry of consequence is exacting and cannot be done on one's own. A man needs his brothers, his fellow explorers, his God.

In this study we are following the counsel given December 27, 1832, "Seek ye diligently and teach one another." Today conscientious ministers of our own church desire to work together to achieve competency in this field. The wise man knows there are no final answers, no single techniques to be printed in a handbook. We mobilize resources and apply them to a specific case.

Today we need to bring together professional resources and use them with pastoral insights. The day of hit-and-miss treatment is passing. The expectancy of ten-minute solutions is fading. Charles William Stewart puts it this way, "The days of the 'lick-and-a-promise' session with a couple to be married and of the solemn prayer and little else over the quarreling couple are rapidly drawing to a close."

This field of premarital counseling is to be seen as an integral part of family life education, in the total educational program of the church. We are seeing that the better the total program, the less will be the emphasis on any short-time before-marriage interviewing. The necessary inner developments and the greater insights into marriage and family life require a long time for maturing. Yet there will ever be place for the before-the-wedding interview.

Such Is Counseling

Counseling is, was, and shall be. Sometimes it is discussed and emphasized today as if it were a passing fad.

But it is more than a contemporary educational gimmick. As long as there have been human beings there has been counseling. It continues because persons need it and want it. We are not endeavoring to bring in something new: we want to do a better job of what we have been doing for a long, long time.

"Counsel" is an oft-recurring word in scriptures. The Messiah was to be called "Counselor." A key directive of God is, "Listen to the counsel which I shall give unto you" (Doctrine and Covenants 97:1). Counseling is an assigned function in ministry.

The presumption is that counsel is given when a searcher seeks it. It hardly fits the situation when a self-appointed dispenser of advice moves in on another person and starts to hand forth "counsel" without the request of the recipient. Effective counseling presumes a readiness, a responsiveness on the part of the one to whom counsel is given.

At least two persons are involved in counseling: a counselor and a counselee. The former is presumed to have such experience and insight as will insure competency in the area of consultation. The counselee is presumed to be wanting guidance in some field in which he believes the counselor is qualified to give advice. Some counselees want encouragement, some want assistance, some want the counselor to do their thinking for them and to come up with specific solutions.

The genuine counselor looks to the welfare and development of the counselee and to the good of all concerned. The counselor is not a dispenser of solutions. He is not a judge in the court of personal relationships. He is not a walking encyclopedia, nor a lawbook. He is not an "I'm-telling-you" director. Rather does the counselor endeavor to increase the competency of the counselee for making decisions. He sets out to help the searcher see things more clearly, more comprehensively than he has been seeing them before. This is stated succinctly in *Marriage Counseling: A Casebook* (Abingdon Press, page 31).

"All counseling aims, at least theoretically, at developing insight into the nature of the problem and the causes or factors which produced it; and endeavors to give the counselee support, encouragement, reassurance and new perspective so that he may look upon himself as but one of many who face or have faced similar problems which can be solved under favorable circumstances."

In other words, the counselor aims to help the counselee to see himself, to see others, and to see the total situation in larger light, with clearer perspective. He helps the searcher to increase his competency in decision making. This same text phrases the matter this way in another place: "Marriage counseling does not involve writing prescriptions for unwilling clients but helping them to clarify their feelings, to understand their behavior, and to make their own decisions." The counselor sets himself to create the atmosphere, to mobilize the resources, to enlarge the perspective for accomplishing sound choices.

Let Pastoral Counseling Be Distinctive

There is counseling in many fields. There are vocational counselors, educational counselors, health counselors, finance counselors, psychological counselors, marriage counselors, and more. The pastoral counselor ought to be somewhat at home in all these in order to integrate them. It is likely that a problematical situation in family life may involve every one of these fields. The wise pastoral counselor knows when to refer counselees to specialists in these specialized fields.

Counseling in the name of the church under the auspices of the church ought to involve a "plus" factor. Persons expect and ought to expect a spiritual quality in counseling when ministers serve as counselors. Here are some of the distinctives in pastoral counseling:

1. Pastoral counselors are concerned with the total person and with the "total redemption" of the person.

2. The pastoral counselor will see and evaluate each person in his own right and with his own capacities and will not try to force the person to go where he inwardly is unable to go.

3. The pastoral counselor will see a person or a couple's situation in a larger, continuing, and more inclusive relationship.

4. The pastoral counselor will use the resources of the church, especially the fellowship and schooling of the congregation, as they contribute to the working through of problems and the development of persons.

5. The pastoral counselor will see God in the role of Counselor to the degree that counselees will be inclined and be able to detect and utilize the counselings of God through scriptures, through science, through persons, through communion with God.

6. The ministry of the Holy Spirit is available in the expressions of discernment, faith, love, wisdom, and hope in the ministry of counseling.

The Church's Inclusive Program of Family Life Education

Any counseling before marriage ought to be a part of an inclusive program of family education. Such a program looks to the lifelong span of the person. More and more authorities in education are saying that when this program is conducted effectively there will be less need to crowd in a short-term concentrated course and counseling just before marriage. Most are saying that this is piecemeal and a little late. When education is continuous there is greater likelihood of stable marriage.

Research is disclosing, too, the correlation between sound, happy membership in a family during childhood and youth and prospects for good family living when persons get married. We are seeing that we need to give more attention to youth's participating effectively, and happily in their own family circles rather than to try to "prepare" for some marriage in a future day.

What has happened in family relations of candidates for marriage is of great significance. Education for marriage goes back a long way. Ideas about sex, sense of security or insecurity, feelings of acceptance or rejection, phobias and confidences get their start in earlier years. If there are quirks and twists in persons growing out of their childhood, three or four conferences at the time of marriage are not going to resolve these. Such confusions and conflicts take many sessions and much patience.

Premarital counseling needs to be connected with post-marital counseling. Many problems and strains can be met only as they appear. Previous study will lay foundation for this later counseling. Situations unpredicted may arise. There may be a sudden windfall of money or there may be a health deterioration of either member of the marriage. This education and counseling service ought to continue into senior adulthood. This expectancy ought to be in the thinking of those who plan sessions at the time of marriage.

One of the major factors in family life education is the education of the entire congregation about the nature of and the factors involved in a happy, healthy family association. Even the mind and heart of the congregation will condition the kind of wedding, the expenditures for honeymoon and home, and other needs. More and more we are seeing that family life education involves the life of all the families and the life of the congregation as a family.

Whatever is done in counseling at the time of marriage is to be seen as an integral part of the total congregational program of family life education. Without this larger program the consultations will be limited in effect. In such an inclusive program the counseling will be more effective and will involve less of instructional ministry. Attitudes and values and appreciations ought to be covered in the large, lifelong program.

The desirable situation is for the minister involved in pre-marriage counseling to have a knowledge of the two persons who anticipate marriage. There is merit in continuing home ministry over imported ministry. There is merit in imported ministry when specialists fit into the ongoing educational program of the congregation.

Guidelines Concerning Counseling

These fundamentals apply to all fields of counseling. They are pertinent in pastoral counseling concerning marriage.

1. The place, the surroundings should contribute to the atmosphere of counseling. More and more branches are providing a room for pastoral ministry in the total church plant. A living room with the family coming and going is not a suitable place. The setting ought to contribute to a feeling of relaxation and privacy without being stuffy and "sanctimonious."

2. The conference begins with the life and the personalities of the counselees. No outline can be laid down, nor can an agendum for all couples be drawn up. Persons are not identicals and interpersonal relations are not the same. Sometimes it is advisable to meet the two persons together at first; sometimes it is expedient to meet them separately.

3. The counselor comes with open mind, and with a responsible spirit. He is not inclined toward preconceptions

and ready solutions. He is prepared to discover and formulate decisions accordingly. If he has been closely associated with the couple he would be conversant with their lives. Many of the most intimate matters never come out, however, until persons establish a counseling or confessional rapport.

4. A problem first presented by the counselee is frequently not the most important problem. The problem presented may be selected out of shyness, out of hesitancy to mention the major deep-in-self problem, out of recency of happenings, out of lack of insight, out of endeavor to slant the story. Thus one woman began with a statement of disbelief in God, at least doubt about God, which statement led on to disclosure of troubles growing out of sex irregularities.

5. The counselor stays within the limitations of his experience and competence. He refers matters outside his field of competence to specialists in other fields. The wise minister will refer matters concerning conception and contraception to men of medicine.

6. Listening is a major part of the consulting process. The man who cannot listen can never counsel. Listening discovers attitudes as well as facts. The counselor can guide the conversation to which he listens.

7. The counselor leads the counselee to develop his own plans rather than plan for him. He may suggest alternatives. He will point out factors and merits of plans. He will throw light on proposals. The decisions are those of counselees.

8. Each person or each couple are pictured in terms of their total backgrounds and environment, their cultural backgrounds, their childhood and youth, their worlds of values, their religious thought and practices and affiliations. The counselor endeavors to get a complete rounded-out picture of the situation.

9. Highly important are the pictures the persons have of the kind of family life, the kind of association they want, the values esteemed for family living. A basic question is, what is wanted out of life together? Children? Homeownership? Life in a congregation? Education? Travel? Other?

10. The counselor is humble. He does not see himself as endowed with powers of omniscience. One wise counselor prayed each morning that he might resist the temptation to play God and prayed each evening for forgiveness for having succumbed to the temptation. The counselor believes God will guide him but does not believe he himself holds a monopoly on this guiding.

HELPS ON METHODS IN COUNSELING

The relationship between counselor and counselee is recognized as central in the counseling process. There has to be a close understanding, a development of confidence if the counseling is to be successful. There is no place for preaching or prying. The counselor is on the same plateau as the counselees. He is not on a high throne looking down at suppliants. He is a friend to those who come to a man who they believe can and will understand and guide. Those who are going to talk about marriage will be talking about the most intimate relationship known to men, and this calls for trust and empathy.

Broadly speaking, we think of counseling as falling into two types, the nondirective and the directive. The distinction is made here for clarification. In directive counseling the counselor tends to tell persons what to do, to give answers, to point the way to go. In nondirective counseling the counselee is the active agent. It is he who endeavors to discover, to define, to diagnose the problem and the situation, specific and general, and who works through to a solution. In all this the counselor functions as a catalyst helping to interpret what the counselee brings forth, and enabling him to draw on his own and other resources for the solution of his problem. The counselor maintains the atmosphere of learning together with God.

Sometimes there is need for directive counseling. There are cases of emergency when information has to be given at once, when time is precious, and when some answers have to be made for the present. Sometimes practical help has to be given in order to make possible the continuing counseling which will develop the needed foundation for living with one's self as well as with one's partner and with one's associates. Sometimes a minister counsels with a couple for the first time after invitations to their wedding have been mailed out. Only a few weeks remain before the wedding. There is not time to build up the insights, the community that will be needed for wholesome married life. Attention has to be given to arrangements for the wedding, to procuring medical examination and license, to plans for a wedding trip, and to housing. The deeper matters of their own personalities, their own theologies, their own values cannot be covered in so short a time. These ought to have been in the educational program months before. The counselor has to do the expedient thing. He will point to post-marriage education that he realizes should have been going on before the wedding.

Here are some of the basic fields to be explored in counseling about marriage. These are fields the counselor will have in mind. They will not always follow the order mentioned here. On the whole the first ones are good starters. No fixed order in an agendum for counseling is advisable. Persons and couples do not have identical backgrounds or identical needs.

1. Move into a who-is-who conversation. This will bring out the identity of persons, their general backgrounds, their

occupational patterns, and other significant helps. This is basic. However, it should be conversational and not cross-questioning. The counselor can point up interesting items and express appreciation for things well done. For instance, a young man was required to assume the responsibility of providing for his mother and two younger members of the family when his father died. This cut short his educational planning but it gave him sound experience in getting and holding a job and in managing money. The counselor was wise enough to see that this experience might be an asset or liability or both. The man felt at ease as the counselor commended him for what he had done. He kept this in mind for further conversation.

2. Discover how the two persons met; find out what drew them together and how they became engaged. The alert counselor will find in this conversation clues to their interests, to their type of social expression, to community of interests or to lack of this, and much more. Books might be written on "How We Met" and the content could be very revealing. One couple met on city tennis courts. One was a member and one a nonmember. A relaxed conversation about this brought about an at-home-ness on the part of the man, a nonmember. It brought out many essentials. A couple met in the dinner line of General Conference and went to church together that night. The conversation brought out the nature of the interests of both of them in the life of the church. One couple met on a commercial dance floor. She was a member but was not involved. As she said, "My name was on the records." He had no church connection or association. The story of their going to church together for the first time and of the reaction of both of them toward the small, friendly congregation opened a narration that told ever so much about their plans and their outlooks.

3. Look to the educational, vocational, residential expectations and plans after marriage. This involves "what we want to do" and "what we can do." Today it is highly important that a couple face the changing that is going on in the industrial, agricultural, and professional fields of living. A couple are quite unprepared to face tomorrow if they do not look into the changes and transitions that are taking place. Every lasting vocation calls for continuing education. This may be "on the job training." One couple wisely included in their plans the requirement that in his electrical installation work he would be going to school one night a week and would be studying one night a week for some time to come. All this needs to be seen together. The exploration can be interesting and stimulating.

4. Consider their attitudes toward their own families, their own parents, the ways of life in their families, the likes and the dislikes involved. This will not be disclosed in a few minutes. Sometimes this will require several interviews. Facts alone will not be enough. It is necessary to see the person as a child and as a youth in the family relationship. Some attachments may be discovered. Some tensions may remain. This is not a matter of reviving the past; it is a matter of discovering the past on which the future family life is going to be constructed.

5. Look to the things they have in common in recreational activities, in social contacts, in life interests. There ought to be joint likes and interests and also some differences. The first can provide community; the second can provide richness through diversity. The counselor will note whether differences will be promoting breaches and conflicts or richer family living as each brings in his or her world of interest. If he is a golf enthusiast and she lets slip that she considers him a "nut" on golf and golfing a nuisance, there is place for consideration before too late. If

she likes Beethoven and he wants bebop, there needs to be some understanding and maybe some meeting on "Seventy-six Trombones." With all this goes a philosophy of social and recreational life that needs to be shared, that needs to be well visioned. With the reduction of employment hours this is going to be increasingly important.

6. Explore the attitudes toward children in the home-to-be. This includes motivations for wanting children or not wanting children. To want children is not enough. Some parents-to-be want children chiefly for their own self-centered, self-satisfying interests. The ideas of the role of the child, the association with the child, the discipline of the child are of great consequence. Once in counseling a couple it was discovered that he did not want to have any children. In time he divulged the fact that he had come from a family of nine children with a meager income and inadequate housing. His picture of children involved dirty clothing, wrangling at meals, running noses, and raucous voices. He had been an older child and had had to take care of younger brothers and sisters. It was arranged for this couple to visit in homes where children were clean and affable, where they were interested in diverse activities, and where they could converse. Gradually the picture in his mind changed. He wanted children, and had them. Here is a case where three or four sessions just before marriage could not have resolved the problem.

7. Bring out their ideas about sex, about sex practices. Sometimes this counseling may be held in separate sessions. This would be the case if one or the other were tied in knots about something and could not speak out. In time they need to converse together. Their backgrounds may have led on one side to notions of the evil nature of sex with consequent feelings of fear, hostility, and guilt and on the other side to notions of relaxed sexual indulgence. It is regrettable that often these notions do not come to the fore

until many years after marriage. The couple have not previously been able to bring these matters out for discussion. The general counsel is that sex is not to be discussed as a separate compartment of living but as an essential part of the total person and is ever to be related to the total personhood and familyhood. Much of this cannot be accomplished in a few sessions if no previous background has been built up.

8. Ascertain whether they are able to converse about matters of faith and church allegiance. One of the most unwise notions is, "Everything will work out all right." It is postulated that if they love each other, there will be no problems. If a couple cannot and will not converse about matters of theology, of personal faith, of church membership before they are married, they are not going to find some suddenly realized ability to do so after marriage. This applies to those who belong to the same church, to those who have membership in the Reorganized Church of Jesus Christ of Latter Day Saints. The counselor will endeavor to ascertain *whether* they talk and *how* they talk and *what* they talk about.

9. Examine the evaluation and appreciation of the one person for the other. This is more than a rating-scale operation. This is more than a likes-and-dislikes listing. This is an endeavor to see the person as a whole. Marriage calls for a frank, honest appraisal of one's self and of one's partner. This will include the realization of inadequacies and peculiarities, but it will emphasize adequacies and appealing qualities. A sense of humor and ability to imagine are indispensable in this operation. This exploration sees a person as he is and it involves getting hold of an image of potentials yet to develop to bring to pass the person and partner that is to be. If there is discounting of one by the other, if there is intent to dominate, if there is disposition to use one as means for elevating the other then the

counseling is coming pretty late.

10. Examine the evaluation and appreciation of the one person for the other person. Sometimes the picture of the other is fanciful and unreal, sometimes too low or too partial, sometimes denunciatory in part or in the whole picture. Those who plan to associate in family living need to learn to see things as they are and also as they can become. There should be recognition of inadequacies but the emphasis should be on adequacies and appealing characteristics. Said one woman, "I have a wart and my friends are aware of this, but I would not want a friend to so concentrate on this that she would see nothing more." A fair, inclusive, honest, considerate picturing of the partner in marriage is indispensable. Sometimes achieving this takes a long while. This training in evaluating others should precede counseling about marriage. Often it does not come until a husband and wife have lived together for several years.

11. Consider together the way of looking into the future. If one or both persons come hopelessly or fatalistically or indifferently into the future, there is little hope for the marriage. If a couple says, "If we do not make a go of it, we can get a divorce," they ought not marry. If they say, "We hope we can hold out until Jesus comes," they ought not marry. If they say, "What can we expect in a world such as this for ourselves and our children?" they ought not marry. There are many kinds of hope, ranging from shallow dreaming through childish wishing through plans to make sound purposes come true. Couples will do well to join with Pierre Teilhard de Chardin when he says, "The whole future of the Earth, as of religion, seems to me to depend on the awakening of faith in the future." This kind of faith gets into the basic theology of persons. Such a theology is constructed over a long period of time. This cannot be formulated in three or four sessions with a

counselor. This is part of the longtime training before engagement and lifelong training after marriage.

QUESTIONS, SITUATIONS THAT CONCERN COUPLES

Here are some fields in which couples or one member of a marriage partnership may make inquiries. The list does not include the total range of inquiries. It does express the wide range of topics that arise either before or after marriage. Some that come up after marriage should have been considered months before marriage. These depict pretty well the complex mosaic of living.

1. CULTURAL DIFFERENCES

These differences may rise out of diversity in national and sectional backgrounds. When a Jew and a non-Jew meet and marry, two cultures are meeting. This involves menus, observance of festivals, literature, and more. It takes more than a stated intent to take up the culture of another person: one slowly grows into the new culture. After years of marriage a wife who loved her husband could say, "I still detest the smell of sauerkraut." A wife said she felt out of place with her husband's family in their Italian culture.

2. EDUCATIONAL BACKGROUNDS

This raises problems of communication; it also may bring up attitudes toward self and toward the partner in marriage. A man who had not finished high school confided after some years of marriage that he felt inferior to his wife in education and resented it. She had had three years of college. The two can become aware of differences, can endeavor to understand and to smile. If the educational differences are pronounced the hurdle may be too great. The difference may rise out of fields of specialization. A woman who majors in social philosophy and a man who majors in accounting may need to search a common ground. A woman of limited education admitted she felt out of place with her husband and his people. She said, "They're at home with Plato and Poe—I can't get above pancakes." A counseling session a week or so before marriage is quite late to look at this.

3. ATTITUDES TOWARD FAMILY BACKGROUNDS.

One member may be proud of his family background while another is ashamed of it. This is not to say that there ought to be pride or shame: it is saying that this is a reality. A young man came out of a Polish background in a large city. He was ambitious and went on to a large university for his bachelor's degree and then on to another for his degree in law. His parents remained in their Polish sector and maintained their Polish ways. He would not take his wife to his parental home and he did not want his parents to visit his American home in a suburban area. Jane Addams once met such a situation by bringing an Italian mother into Hull House in the presence of the youth and praising the quality of her handmade lace. It was a revelation to the youth to discover that the Italian mother could do something that would elicit the commendation of Miss Addams. This kind of attitude about one's family can lie buried in a person so that it is brought to the fore with reticence.

4. INDIVIDUAL AND FAMILY FRIENDSHIPS AND ASSOCIATIONS

One couple in considering their future marriage asked this significant question, "Does each one keep the pre-marriage friends or do we develop a new circle of common friends?" An unfortunate thing about their pre-marriage association was that they had been so enamored with each other that they had not associated with other couples. Even in the congregation they had kept to themselves, had sat together in church, and had walked out without association with others. Another unfortunate situation is the living of the two persons in such unrelated vocational, recreational, and social circles that they have two unrelated worlds. Such couples may find themselves stranded for friends. The counseling ought to have been done a long time before. The problem needs a foundation of a sound philosophy of friendship and the cultivation process for meritorious friendships. Life well lived in the church should provide these common associations. The well-balanced husband has friends of his own and he has friends in a circle with his wife. The two ought to be complementary. The normal man needs both. The wife is self-centered and shortsighted who wants to monopolize her husband's time. This applies in the same way to the other side of the family.

5. RELATION TO RELATIVES

This may involve the in-laws of the partner or the blood-relatives of the person's own family. Arrangements range from proximity in residence, through times and nature of visiting, through family subsidy, to caring for and controlling children. Sometimes it involves attachment to or resistance to one or more parents. In unusual yet not uncommon cases it brings in emotional attachment and need for emancipation from parental involvement. In some cases strains come from undue telephoning to a parent, or from continual asking advice about what to do. If this matter has not been brought to the fore until pre-marriage counseling, the remedial program may entail considerable time.

6. CARE OF PARENTS AND OTHER DEPENDENTS

This problem may be declining but it has not disappeared from the picture. One of the couple has been living with a parent. What now? Shall the couple move into the parental home? Or shall the parent be brought into the new home? There is a general rule that no roof is large enough for two families of two generations to live together under it. In the main this is true. But this can hardly sweep aside all situations. The kind of attachment, the kind of motivation for including the parent, the kind of program of employment of the husband and wife, the kind of community among the three are of great consequence. Whatever is decided calls for clear understanding of a program of action and of roles and relationships. One family included a father quite comfortably by providing living room and sleeping quarters with the understanding that at times the family would be having activities and friends that would not be within his interests. Sometimes younger brothers and sisters left without parents are included in the new home. The general guideline is: plan and carry on with insight into the basic integrity of the family and the welfare of the ancillary member.

7. SOCIAL STANDING AND SOCIAL SELECTEES

A couple may differ in this field or they may agree and both be wrong or both be right. This gets at the question of values, of motivations. Every husband and wife must sooner or later face such questions as, What makes a person worthful? On what basis are we going to consider men and women of superior quality? On what basis are we going to select our associates? They may permit the pressures of their social world to determine this without any qualitative thinking on their part. As children come into the home, mothers and fathers will have compelling ideas about the children and the youth with whom they shall associate. For both adults and children the question includes the who and the how of association. This gets into consideration of choosing friends and families who will constitute the circle of family friends. This has to do with friends in the church as well as out of the church. Said one couple, "We want to have some stimulating and socially agreeable friends who are members of the church but we do not want to be snobbish and over-selective." What shall be the range of contacts? And what shall be the basis?

8. GIVING OF GIFTS, SENDING OF GREETINGS

Differences arise out of monetary considerations and out of closeness of family connections. There is a wide range of difference in this matter. In some families the giving of gifts is prominent in the group relationships. In other families giving is at a minimum. If two persons marry who come from these divergent patterns sooner or later the matter will become a problem. It should be discussed before there is a domestic eruption. This should be noted a long time before marriage. Remarked one husband, "If one of Mary's relatives sneezes, she has to send a get-well card." Said a wife about birthday observances in her husband's family, "A birthday celebration is an all-out affair. Everybody comes and everybody brings gifts. And the gifts do not come from the dime store. Our budget will not take the strain." She did not know how to get at the problem without seeming to be a non-appreciating rebel. One husband was annoyed again and again by his wife who watched closely to discover the price and quality of gifts received so that she might give accordingly. He said she had reduced giving to a bargain-counter arrangement. Certainly a budget ought to include something about the amount that can be spent on gifts. The annual budget ought to give consideration to allotment for such happenings, within reason. Often some insight is needed into personal relations of high calibre that do not demand burdensome exchanging of gifts and greetings.

9. ABILITY AND INABILITY TO COMMUNICATE CLEARLY AND COMFORTABLY

This is a number-one problem today. Usually when a

wife says that her husband does not talk or a husband says the same about the wife this is no recent development. Sometimes while dating couples fail to develop the art of communicating about things necessitating communication. They just go places together and rely on manual conversation. Sometimes one tries to induce the other to talk while the one so influenced responds by "clamming up." The counselor needs to distinguish between the person who does not know how to speak forth and the person who deliberately plans to say nothing. This situation requires quite a long course in exploring persons and understanding them. Facilitation rather than compulsion is the way to go. One requisite stands forth: those who converse must have something worth conversing about, and must have a two-way sharing in this field. Monologue is not conversation. If both are interested, it is likely that they will talk. Couples need to do things together so they can talk about things together.

10. MOODS AND MOOD EXPRESSION

"Moods" constitute a major consideration in marital counseling. One wife asserted frankly when asked what troubled her most, "If I just knew what mood he was going to be in when he came home, and why he was in it, I would know what to do." A husband poured out this admission, "She has always been moody but now that she is in the menopause I don't know whether I can take it." The interview revealed that both husband and wife were uninformed about the biological and psychological nature of the menopause. It is not uncommon to find both rather hazy about aspects of the menstrual periods. All of us need insight into what we mean by moods and into factors that cause them. We need some insights into the spiritual hygiene of planning to live in the rhythm of feelings and to ride the emotional waves. We need to understand ourselves and each other. When a prosaic husband with few emotional intensities mates with a wife who can be charted in ups and downs, the two are likely to have misunderstandings. All husbands and wives need the gospel of good spiritual health. This schooling should precede marriage.

11. LANGUAGE AND VOICE CONTROL

In the larger sense this has to do with what is said and how it is said. One counselor of wide and long experience said he believed that every candidate for marriage ought to be required to take a course "in voice control and modulation." Voice quality, he said, can create a home atmosphere that can irritate or inspire to good. Observed one counselor, "If I had to listen to her penetrating, raucous voice screeching at husband and children without saying anything of consequence, I think I would spend my life out-of-doors." On the other side came this comment concerning a husband, "His inarticulate grunts and belly-aching tone of voice would make any wife a bundle of nerves." Recently along the street a young mother yelled at her small boy in a shrill, high-pitched voice with a belligerent tone. Her threat, "Come here or I'll knock your block off." The child did not get the full import of the remark, but he yapped back in the same voice quality. The situation involves having something worth saying, a healthy motivation for saying it, and the art of saying it with clarity and gentility. The solution does not always mean keeping quiet. Sometimes it does. The other extreme is cultivating a superficial way of speaking that voices little or no sincerity. The words of the wise man are still valid, "Out of the mouth the heart speaketh."

12. READING MATERIALS AND PATTERNS OF READING

What a family reads, what it thinks as it reads, what it does after reading constitute a meaningful criterion of the fellowship of the family. Every couple getting married should spend one council session on what they are going to be reading. This includes what they are going to have on hand for reading and how they are going to be reading. Often such comments as these are expressed after some time of married life together: "He [or she] simply never reads anything." "What he [or she] reads is not very good material." "He gets home and becomes antisocial while he reads the papers." Such a list of comments might be extended. Some church-minded couples set up the "three standard books" as their reading diet. Some read separately but never together and never converse about their readings. In one family the husband is a very slow reader and the wife a rapid reader. He is self-conscious about his rate of reading and will say little or nothing about what he reads. When ordained to the priesthood he became even more self-conscious. Some couples get into marked differences about reading in bed. Friends ought to get some understanding on this matter before they become engaged—certainly before they get married.

13. TELEVISION AND RADIO SCHEDULING

This involves both when and what and how. Sometimes a wife, sometimes a husband may be described as a TV addict. This may mean longtime listening to whatever may be on or it may be limited observance of a few favored programs. There are differences on volume. One husband observed, "When it is bedtime I want that television or radio turned off." And the wife replied, "Not in the middle of a program." Scheduling of radio and television gets at the cultivation of tastes and the appetite for materials. Educators in the field of family living say frankly that the broadcasting materials can be asset or liability. They can limit or expand. It is imperative that husband and wife and children work out a program with mutual consideration and with awareness of what the materials are doing to them as persons and as a family.

14. ATTIRE AROUND THE HOUSE

Shall we dress in negligee? Or in "casuals"? Or in ready-for-visitors attire? More than one family has gone to battle over this or retired into a time of truce. Such items as this come up: If one takes off shoes, does one also take off hose or socks? In some camps the answers are definite. Is breakfast eaten in get-out-of bed attire? More than one husband asks, "Do I have to keep looking at those curlers?" And the wife asks, "What about shaving?" A husband and wife trying to find some common ground observe, "Maybe we should buy some clothes just for wearing around the house." One wife remarks, "He has an athletic physique. If he is going to show it, I wish he would get some walking shorts." In such cases it is usually discovered that there is wide difference in background attitudes toward the human body, the line between privacy and public appearance, the wearing of clothing by small children, nudity, and more. These matters get into the theology and social theories of persons. There are no five-minute answers.

15. FOODS AND SERVICE OF MEALS

This is more than a joking about what to eat. Likes and dislikes and prejudices for and against and family heritage get into this. A long time ago a lecturer on family living said that many a family starting out gets into a dither over gravy. Right. Is it to be thin and soupy or thick and "puddiny" as it comes to the table? Does the new bride have to be taught gravy making by mother? This typifies many potential causes of strains. What is cooked and how it is served matter tremendously in many families. How the table is prepared enters in, too. How the food is served and consumed are part of the story. Said one bride, "If he eats that way again, I'll scream." Much of this is not discussed. The participants give emotional vent or say nothing. The counselor can enable the two to learn how to converse and how to develop a working program. A good sense of humor will help. The situation is complicated if the husband is skilled in cooking and the wife is inexperienced. One husband smiled when he said he looked at the cooking of his bride and felt to say, "Forgive us our trespasses." Certainly the two should never air grievances and dislikes in front of guests and relatives. Sometimes the amateurs have to learn how to live for both food and fellowship.

16. PROGRAM OF SOCIO-RECREATIONAL ACTIVITIES

This consideration is inclusive. It brings in returning home from the day's work and the use of time for reading the papers or for conversing or for picnicking. Some members of the family want free time to themselves. A wife who has been home may resent her husband's reading the paper and may insist that he converse with her. Counseling should guide in laying the general situation on the table with recognition of guiding principles. This includes some philosophy of leisure activities in their relation to personality fulfillment and life values. Then should come the application to formulating a program for this specific couple. The extending of interests would enter in. This puts the matter on a wider basis than asking, Shall we play this game together or alone? Shall we take up swimming together?

17. STARTING THE DAY AND CLOSING THE DAY

These two times call for "the fine art of living together." A couple can blunder into a day and can collapse out of it. The good day ought to be a cooperative taking off and shared rounding out. It is wise that members understand the body makeup of each other. Some persons get out of bed with a zip and are ready to go. Others say they have to warm up the engine. Our body chemistries are not identical. Occasionally both individuals start the day on slow tempo. Both understand and they get along happily. Couples have conferred with me in which one began the day full of energy, ready to go, while the other required time to get going. At first there was resentment on both sides. When they came to recognize their diversity, they planned their mornings accordingly and got along very well. Some persons are "going high" at ten o'clock while others are tired. One wife learned to plan her day so that she would have some reserve of energy and good cheer for closing out the day. Sometimes it is not so much a matter of body chemistry and organic condition. Rather one or the other falls into the habit of being lazy, of reading the newspaper and falling asleep. One husband confided that he did this and thought that he would round everything out by giving his wife a kiss when he got up to wander to bed. The beginning and the closing of the day afford good occasion for conversation, for looking ahead, for shared devotions. There is something pragmatic in the statement, "Start and close the day together with God."

18. EXPRESSION OF AFFECTION

Differences may be articulated before marriage, shortly after marriage, and sometimes not for quite a while. This gets at the nature of wholesome love. For some who are schooled largely by movies and pictures and thin novels the romantic way of life calls for "heavy" and continuing love-making of the movie-screen type. Most of these notions are shallow and self-defeating. They get nowhere in home building. On the other hand are the prosaic patterns of the daily round out of which anything that suggests "having a date" and expressing affection are dropped out.

Considerations in this field call for conceptions of the nature and the role of love in the maturing person. It calls for interpretation of love in which two persons are looking together in the same direction rather than gazing at each other. Enduring love calls for persons doing significant things together. Genuine love calls for looking together with God and doing together with God. Backgrounds differ concerning expression of affection. The range runs all the way from staid to "sloppy" patterns. One wife wanted no expression in public, so when her husband returned after more than a year's absence in the military, she expected to shake hands. He grabbed her in an affectionate embrace. She was perturbed that her hair got mussed and that all the warm greeting was rather "public." Sometimes the counselor has to be quite discerning to detect all this and to guide the considerations.

19. THEORIES ABOUT SEX AND SEX EXPRESSION

Some couples achieve a common understanding in these matters. Others may drag on through the years without understanding and without the ability to converse. Not infrequently after ten or twenty years of married life couples will come for counsel on matters that ought to have been considered in their childhood and youth. These matters should be included in the church's total educational program and should precede pre-marriage counseling. A couple who had been married fifteen years discovered that she had come to marriage with a sense of the impurity of sex and of disinclination to engage in sex expression. She felt that the Bible advised that the wife should "submit" to the husband, so she had done so unwillingly. He also held the idea that it was the wife's duty to "submit" to the wishes of the husband and so felt that there was nothing to talk over. A crisis brought them for counsel and the clarification of the longstanding problem. Another wife believed that sexual intercourse was for procreative purposes only. Great tensions rose out of the contrasting attitudes. There are ever so many theories and attitudes with ascetic denial at one extreme and continuing indulgence at the other. If there are such attitudes, they will not be cleared up in two or three pre-marriage counseling sessions. If such attitudes are discovered just before marriage, the counseling should continue after the marriage.

20. ETHICS AND PRACTICES IN BIRTH CONTROL

Every couple needs to do some cooperative thinking in this field. Many will need the assistance of counselors. The counselor will need to be considerate and helpful. I find that many persons need help to open the subject. The minister will need to understand the language and the concerns of each person. Several have asked, "Is it right?" and "What does the church have to say about this?" One conscientious husband confided that after the birth of seven children he had practiced birth control but always with a troubled conscience. It is likely that some of the discussion in this area will be loaded with prejudices and wishes. There is need to recognize differences in motivation and conditions. Some look to preventing pregnancy. Sometimes health conditions enter in. Some consider they should do their part in reducing the population explosion. Some want freedom from anxiety. We cannot put everyone into a single category. We need to get hold of the factors and the attitudes and the backgrounds involved. The counselor can help counselees to see the entire program from psychological, biological, social, and theological considerations. Always we ought endeavor to help inquirers to rise above the latest fads, quack solutions, and treatments. We point to sound counsel by competent doctors of medicine and others.

21. CHILD-BEARING AND CHILD-REARING

One couple says that pregnancy is a nuisance; another says it is a source of joy and pride and promise. If husband and wife have contrasting attitudes, strains follow. One couple said that the wife looked upon child-bearing as the painful consequence of sin while the husband viewed it about as he would a cow bearing a calf out in the pasture. They did not get together on the matter until years after marriage. One man came from a home in which the father had been a tyrant, exacting and unreasonable, so he determined not to discipline his son at all. His wife had come from a family in which there was a blending of consistent discipline and understanding love. They had never mentioned this field in their marriage plans. Here is a place for happy exploration together. A couple may need to build up a vocabulary for such exploration.

22. THE NATURE AND THE USE OF SCRIPTURES

Divergence in interpreting and using the scriptures can split a family wide open. One may hold the scriptures to be the inerrant word of God that give specific solutions for all problems of living. This is especially marked if the Bible is considered the one and only word of God. The other member may see the Bible as the record of man-God relations with relativity involved in insight and in writing. For such a person the Bible becomes a guide for living rather than a lawbook. Then there is the person who considers the Bible as folklore, interesting and useful but not authoritative. Often such questions are avoided before marriage and cause mounting confusion in the business of living after marriage. Add to this the belief in the Book of Mormon and the Doctrine and Covenants and the confusion can increase or use of the scriptures can enrich. It makes considerable difference whether the Book of Mormon is considered a manual for archaeological pursuits, a finalized edition of the gospel, or a witness of the universal Christ. The Doctrine and Covenants can be taken as a source book for legalistic use in beliefs and practices or as a collection of counsels that are to be interpreted in their historical settings. One husband confided, "I am tired of hearing, Thus saith the Books!" One wife admitted, "My husband would have us chew our food with the Word of Wisdom."

23. CONCEPTION OF GOD AND OF GOD'S EXPECTANCIES

This is at the heart of good family living. How God is thought of as operating in his universe, as relating himself to persons matters ever so much. The couple concerned with lining up with God, in loving with God, in laboring with God will have a program of contacting and communing that differs greatly from the ways of a couple who think of cajoling, almost bribing God to get him on their side and to get from him what they want. The couple who think of living righteously "together with God" will have a program quite different from that of persons who see little or no link between righteous living and what they call worship. In one interview a counselor said very directly, "You are wanting to give full time to God, but you cannot work with him until you come to discover what God is setting out to do. Thus far you are concerned with being busy. But to what purpose?" The couples with penetrating insight want to be working with God in the developing of their home, in all phases of family living. This is basic in counseling before and after marriage. This is the core of family life education.

24. BASICS FOR ETHICS

Every person, every couple, every family faces the need to identify the foundation by which ethical judgments are made. What constitutes rightness? In our modern mutable society with new situations arising all the time we cannot rely on a catalogued listing of what is right and what is wrong. The line between white and black is not distinct. Some social situations have never occurred before. This means that modern Latter Day Saints must be schooled in the making of moral judgments. Often two persons arrange to get married without exploring this field. One family experienced serious strains when one held to the basis, "My grandfather, an elder, says . . ." and the other sought a scriptural quotation to support every act. Interpretations often clashed. Today a couple need to be able to sit in council and identify in the nature of God and in the nature of God's universe the basis of choice making. One of the requisites for marriage is experience and insight in problem solving on a God-based ethic. One couple had to make a decision concerning a Caesarian operation. It became a matter of rightness of such procedure and they had no sound way of making the needed moral judgment. Another couple went into panic over the rightness or wrongness of a hysterectomy. Another couple faced the question of dancing and did not know how to attack the question. Couples should recognize differences in their approach to ethical questions and the need to establish some basis for making moral judgments.

25. RACE AND RACE RELATIONS

Today this question is inescapable. What a family is going to think and do in this matter is unavoidable. It becomes more so as children live in the home. No one can give a worked-out, inherited program. Each couple has to explore the situation and formulate a program of action. Today this calls for some clear thinking and some wide overviewing. One couple came to a seeming impasse. He worked in construction with Negroes of limited slanting toward productive labor. He endured them in a resentful way. She worked in a school system with Negro teachers of high cultural calibre and with children from stable Negro homes. The two struck fire as they considered what the church in their city should be doing with the Negro. Their discussions became heated arguments. They were unaccustomed to working on such problems. They threw likes and dislikes, prejudices and distorted statistics at each other. Couples ought to experiment in working out differences in thinking on such social questions. In right attitude they can expect insight to develop. They can consider such questions in light of God's mission.

26. ESCHATOLOGY AND DAILY LIVING

This comes up rather often among our people in these contemporary days. Eschatology has to do with "last things." Latter Day Saints can get involved in speculation and in anxiety about what is going to happen. There can be emphasis on "terrible things coming on the earth." There can be speculation and designation about the time of the Second Coming. There can be specific programming about what the family is to do in getting ready for these impending happenings, as judgments on the wicked. A mood of apprehension can develop. Some young couples confide that they wonder if they should bring children into such a world of evil and turmoil. A few couples have wondered if they should purchase or build a house at all in the light of impending disaster. Some have given themselves to building up food supplies. Some have become worried at reports of the letting loose of devilish machinations. It is quite clear that there is a relationship between a family's mood and motivation and their functional eschatology. Some become fearful, some fatalistic, some indifferent, and some speculative. All this stems from the kind of theology the persons have been developing through the years. Young couples need a sound approach to what is taking place in the world. There is little hope for the couple who confided that they wanted to get married this summer and have some time together for they did not expect the world to be standing a year from now.

27. CHURCH MEMBERSHIP AND PARTICIPATION IN CHURCH LIFE

Sometimes this has to do with membership in different churches. Sometimes neither a prospective husband or wife will belong to a church. Counseling experiences disclose that often an inadequate job is done in this field. The essential is that those considering marriage should be able to disclose their views and loyalties to each other with clarity, with conviction, and with cooperation. It is imperative that the two be able to explore constructively. Postponement is ill-advised. If there is dogmatism and inconsiderateness before marriage, this may be augmented at a later time. Such conversation should be started early in friendly association. When both belong to the same church, the Reorganized Church of Jesus Christ of Latter Day Saints or others, there is need to ascertain what membership in the church entails. There are cases of a wife or a husband wanting the partner to be baptized into "my church." When this has happened, the member often has resented the convert's interest and involvement. How and how much the husband and wife intend to participate are to be considered. A young man ordained came to marriage with intent to participate extensively in the ministerial life of the church, but he said never a word about all this. After a bursting forth in which she "spoke her piece," she asked him, "What am I to do? Just look on? Can we not get into this together?"

28. FAMILY DEVOTIONS

Many couples who seem adverse to providing for some

form of family worship simply do not know how to go about initiating and conducting such. Honest couples often say they are willing to pray together but they must have something about which to pray. This is a credit to their insight and honesty. Persons cannot commune with God unless they have something about which to converse. This means that praying should be related to what the family is doing with God. Without this active expression praying becomes a round of phrasings and praisings that mean little. The counseling pastor can guide the family in what they will be doing together that will constitute something worth talking about with God. Many couples appreciate help in procuring literature that can be shared in a devotional way. Let it be assumed that more families will worship together if they are working together with God in significant service and learning.

29. USE OF TOBACCO AND INTOXICATING BEVERAGES

This is more of a problem than is commonly supposed. Some consider this from the standpoint of "principle," others from the standpoint of "practice." Some say they do not care to smoke or drink but that they want freedom to do so if they wish. In some homes smoking visitors provoke tension. Are ashtrays to be provided? Husbands and wives have differed strongly on this point. If the husband or the wife is involved in business and social situations, what of the cocktail? There are also tea and coffee tensions. Often these questions are not considered objectively with honest attempt to set a basis for action. Too often the conversation becomes a meeting of prejudices. What is to be the course if one smokes and the other does not? The couple may need help in getting such matters on the table for wise analysis.

30. PRE-MARRIAGE HAPPENINGS IN PRIVATE LIVING

Do you think I should tell him [or her]? How often counselors hear this question. Somewhere in the life of the bride-to-be or the husband-to-be things have happened that they wish had not happened. This is more frequent than many presume. Often there have been sexual intimacies. Sometimes there have been drinking episodes with attending misconduct. Sometimes there have been brushes with the law. The conscientious person may have a sense of guilt before God and a sense of infidelity in the company of friends, especially with the fiancé or fiancée. Here again there is no single answer. Certainly the person needs to get right with God. Some things done in private may well remain in private. Here is a situation in which the counselor will need to be very understanding and very close-mouthed. In one situation both confessed to the counselor their own shortcomings and indiscretions. It seemed wise for the two to speak to one another. This they did with the help of the counselor. One was relieved and reached out understandingly to the other. The other, however, began to formulate an attitude of unreliability and infidelity. The wise leadership of the counselor helped to resolve the threatened breach. He continued in his role until the two established a stronger foundation than they had had before.

31. FINANCIAL ADEQUACY AND ASSURANCE

One member of the contracting marriage may want a cash reserve in the bank, some insurance policies, and reasonably sure employment. The other may literally "trust to each day" with "no thought for the morrow." This matter calls for sitting around a council table and considering quite objectively what constitutes reasonable financial security. Many a woman wants to see that her husband has enough earning power, continuity in employment, and pattern of saving to make him a good risk for marriage. Sometimes one or the other can be so insistent on adequate financial security that the marriage should be postponed until he or she can study the way through. If no common consent is reached, there is likely to be anxiety and even taunting after marriage.

32. FAMILY BUDGETING AND RECORD KEEPING

Some newlyweds move into this rather readily. Some couples find this a source of confusion and strain through the years. Many couples never get a theory and a program for doing this. For some it becomes slave-driving labor. For some it becomes a meeting of a legalistic requirement of the church. Some sense the "have-to" without getting the "want-to" and the "know-how." Often one of the two has a bent in this direction, a liking for figures and accounts, while the other avoids money management if it is at all possible. One wife likes to account for every penny while her husband is irked at all this and would rather make general estimates. They have never acquired a common language. Schooling in this field calls for insight into stewardship and personal responsibility. This calls for a theology of stewardship as well as techniques in recording and estimating. This theology must touch the business of living.

33. EMPLOYMENT OF THE WIFE AND USE OF HER INCOME

To work or not to work? This is a persistent question. Some come forth with a finished and final answer. The wise counselor avoids this. He sets up general criteria. Then he gets the picture of this particular family, for it needs to be repeated, "Families are not identicals!" Certainly any argument about "everybody's doing it" is unsound and untrue. Some women will make better companions as they continue their vocational work and express themselves in creative, contributive endeavor. Some would be worn out and irritable if they were to do so. If some women work out of the home, they need help with the household tasks. Matters of physical, mental, and spiritual health are involved. When it comes to children, there is primacy for the welfare of the children. Then the couple has to explore as to what will be best for the children. Many mothers and fathers who are with their children hour after hour do not make outstandingly good parents. Often a competent third party is needed to help the husband and wife see all facets of the problem. One thing stands out: when both are employed, only one income should be used for operating expenses. Then if the mother discontinues working, there will be no reduction in the standard of living. The income of the mother may be used for capital investment, for reserves, for education funds, and the like. This problem gets at the question of values. Employment of the mother for "keeping up" and "making headlines" is hardly commendable.

34. BANKING AND SAVING

The financial patterns of persons are revealed in this consideration. The couple who get married with each owing for a car, a television set, a stereo, with several payments yet to be made, start out on a precarious financial base. They are in the red before they get started. The situation might be worse—or better—if one has been a careless spendthrift and the other a careful spender. Thus one member of a couple to be married commented, "We are still young and we don't need to start saving yet," while the other said, "We'd better start a savings fund, even if it is only a token." Understanding about checking accounts is also important. Shall there be one or two? One young husband put his foot down and said, "When you learn something about money management we shall have a joint account." One young wife spoke out, "You would check out everything we have for a new car and leave us nothing for groceries." Of course all this should have been resolved in previous education in finance, but it was not. So the couple face an inescapable question: savings or no savings?

35. INSURANCE, INCLUDING HEALTH INSURANCE

Some persons are insurance poor and some are poor in insurance. In modern times professional insurance agents do not try to oversell. They get the picture of income and related topics, of the size of the family, and endeavor to estimate what program should be carried on in the light of all these factors. Counseling reveals that some persons do not favor insurance since it shows "weak faith in God" and constitutes a "poor investment." Such attitudes must be recognized and honored. Some believe that when a marriage takes place, the husband should continue his insurance and perhaps take out more while the wife should cancel hers. The compensations and insurance provided by employers and by the government enter in. A couple need to sit down at the table and lay their figures before them. If they cannot do this alone, they should request the help of a competent counselor. In the church the bishop and his counselors and representatives are available. This conversation ought to further their common understanding about family financing.

36. CONTINUING EDUCATION

Today many couples consider marriage and continuing education for one or both. Certainly every couple should look to additional schooling for occupational, cultural, or service reasons. If one is to work while the other goes to school, opinions on values and social relationships may need to be discussed if further education is considered as giving superior standing. Some men, because of their background, may find it very difficult to go to school while their wives work. Certainly the matter of postponing having children enters into the picture.

37. HOUSING CONDITIONS, LOCATION OF THE HOME

Often this problem lasts through decades. It may be a matter of the kind of housing the couple want. It may involve proximity to or distance from relatives. Often it involves convenience to employment. It ought to include considerations of church contacts and associations. Sometimes one will want a family house while the other wants an apartment. One may want a city residence while the other wants to live in a small town. The counselor can help the couple to survey the entire situation and to get hold of the functional motivations in contrast to the stated reasons. The mature couple will be conscious of many factors; the immature person will look at one or two that have momentary emotional appeal.

38. HOUSE FURNISHINGS AND DECOR

Three possibilities stand out: The couple can rent a furnished apartment or house, start out with newly purchased equipment, or "inherit" furnishings. Often the situation involves both what we want and how much we can procure now. Consideration should be given to (1) the basic function of house and home, (2) the decorative and artistic scheme, and (3) financial plans for purchasing. Said one husband-to-be, "We started out thinking about a dream cottage; now it looks as if we were looking for a castle in the clouds." Said one bride, "I'd rather use boxes and blankets than bring in the in-laws' wornout furniture." Differences surfaced when he proposed a western plains pattern for the house and she pictured a French Renaissance. The matter had not been considered until just before the wedding. Then it was a little late. Here is a place where a counselor can guide in combining fact, fancy, and function.

39. HOUSEKEEPING

One husband said with a tinge of humor and with a bit of sarcasm, "The gift of housekeeping ought to be named among the gifts of the gospel: it is one of the gifts my wife does not have." He had come from one of those "immaculate" homes in which his mother had been servile to housekeeping. His wife seemed to have neither the knack nor the disposition. It appeared that she could not be bothered by such menial things. The husband was annoyed and at times embarrassed by the casual way she looked at housekeeping. Another husband said his wife had lots of gods in the home. One of these was the floor which was "too precious" for human locomotion. On the other side are comments to the effect that "he never lifts a finger to help around the house" and that "he never seems to notice when I do anything extra to make the house attractive." Conferences indicate that there is considerable divergence and sometimes hostility in theories and in practices in this area. What are the objectives? When is housekeeping meritorious? How is housekeeping related to homemaking? It appears that here is a field for some husband-wife classes in the educational program of the congregation. Ever and anon we need the saying, "It takes a heap o' living in a house to make it home," and what kind of living?

The final section of this chapter endeavors to sum up many of the things already presented. It begins with a resume of guidelines for counseling. Consideration is then given to some specifics regarding counseling sessions or interviews.

An approach to the first interview is presented in some detail. The number of succeeding interviews, their content and approach, will be determined to a large extent by what has been accomplished in the first interview, available time, etc. There is no attempt to present succeeding interviews in detail. Much will depend upon the minister concerned and a number of varying circumstances. The following outline is presented as a guide.

1. Interview One
   The minister discusses the religious nature of marriage as he becomes better acquainted with the couple. A section dealing with the sacramental nature of marriage is included in the chapter on "Planning Your Wedding Service." Discuss this with them as part of this first interview.
2. Interview Two
   The minister discusses their romance, their interests, family relationships, their basic understanding of sex, and the planning of the family. In many instances it is desirable for the minister to see each partner separately for this discussion. Remember that few of us are really competent to counsel in matters of sex. Do not hesitate to refer couples to reliable counseling services such as doctors and family service agencies.
3. Interview Three
   The minister sees the couple together and discusses more completely the planning of a home and family and family expenses.
4. Interview Four
   The minister discusses their common interests, how to resolve conflicts, and their adjustments to marital difficulties. He also discusses the details of the wedding service, referring to the brochure on "Planning Your Wedding Service" which they have received earlier.

Guidelines for Counseling

1. Consider candidates for counseling as persons whose personalities are to be developing throughout life, using inner resources, social resources, and spiritual resources toward realization of fullness of personality.

2. Blend the giving of advice, information, and guidance in the exploration in accordance with the potentials and the needs of counselees.

3. Point toward respect of the personhood of each other in the maturing companionship of marriage.

4. Interpret sex and other bodily expressions in terms of the total person and of other persons involved.

5. Build a wholesome, functional conception of God and his procedures that will promote spiritual health in members of the family.

6. Advise courage to discontinue plans if contracting parties in an engagement come to discover divergence too great for marriage or lead them toward postponement of the marriage until further community is achieved.

7. Interpret marriage as a covenant relationship with both rights and responsibilities on the part of contracting parties. Set forth the opening phrase of the marriage covenant, "You both mutually agree to be each other's companion."

8. Set forth the necessity of achieving enlightened common consent through interaction and communication in which both participate in conference.

9. Portray love as active outreaching in which two persons "look forward in the same direction," finding companionship in common worthful endeavor, with God in the heart of the looking and questing.

10. Include all facets of balanced personhood and of inclusive living in family life with integration and harmony achieved in God.

The First Interview

How to get started is a basic concern in all fields of counseling. It is a person-with-person conference that cannot begin or continue without the counselor and the counselee reaching understanding and rapport. It is important that we guard against what is called "desk psychology" which comes when a desk creates a barrier and promotes a "job interview" atmosphere. Another feeling to be avoided is the "ecclesiastical psychology" in which the minister is on one side and the layman on the other. The meeting and the greeting are of utmost importance. The minister who puts on an act of the hail-fellow-hello type will not gain the confidence and respect of counselees. Nor will the ecclesiastic who is conscious of his ordination win these. The genuineness of the counselor will speak for itself.

After the greetings and the identification of the purpose for meeting the counselor will do well to identify the roles in the interview as those of seeker and helper. The counselors and the counselees are exploring together an important, fascinating field.

Now comes the conversation for identification. Who are these persons? How do they happen to be here? What are their backgrounds? Where and how did they meet? What drew them together? Here is opportunity for a human-interest story. This is no place for cross-examination, no time for prying. The counselor will develop the spirit of getting acquainted, of coming to know rather than of getting some data to put on a record or some witness material for forming a judgment. The pastoral counselor will express a genuine interest. He will move with warmth into the exploration. He will point up items and happenings of interest and significance. He will not have to state that he is interested in them; this interest will radiate.

The counselor will seek to discover the motives for their coming for consultation. He may have to listen carefully to discover this. Some will come because they consider that couples who are going to be married are supposed to interview some minister. This minister may be the one who is going to officiate in their wedding ceremony. It may be another, perhaps a pastor with whom they have lived and will continue to live. There ought to be a better motivation than this. Some couples will come because they feel inadequate for moving into marriage and want to procure help toward a good start. Their interest may be very general; they may not know how to begin the interview. Some will come with some fairly specific questions. These will probably need to be rephrased. It is possible, too, that the stated questions may not be the ones of major concern. These may have to be unearthed. Once in an interview the stated question had to do with something secondary; the man was actually deeply concerned about his sexual potency. This fear had prompted him to back out of two engagements and he was about to back out again. Sometimes the couple come with identifiable concerns. Once a man wanted to be thoroughly honest when a minister of the Reorganized Latter Day Saint Church was going to officiate. He could not accept the Book of Mormon as authentic. Would the wedding ceremony conducted by one of our ministers imply that he believed in the Book of Mormon? The first comment of the counselor was commendation for his spiritual integrity. Probably few consultations would start on this note, but this man was troubled and voiced his concern as soon as the way was opened.

In this first interview two things stand out: the identification of persons and the identification of problems to be considered. This makes an agendum that will not be exhausted in one session. Both items should expand in meetings that follow. The identification of persons is more than getting names and street addresses and ages. It means getting a picture of the two persons. No person is understood apart from his background and the social situation in which he is living. To indicate that Richard Johnson is a member of the church and a deacon is not enough. What is his conception of the church, of church membership, of ordination? It takes association with a man to sense his life. Then comes the identification of the items to be considered. This list will clarify and expand and contract.

There will be a tendency to want to talk about the wedding ceremony, about wedding plans in general. This can be considered in the course of a later interview. But a minister ought not to definitize any order of service until he comes to know the couple. A good theory of marriage, of marriage covenanting, of family living ought to precede outlining the service. The wedding service is theirs, theirs in common. It does not belong alone to the bride or to the bride's parents. That idea of monopoly holds to social exhibits and dramatic displays in weddings; it does not apply to a religious wedding service. If the counseling is well done, there will probably be some development in the thinking of the couple about the wedding service. They will want something that expresses what they believe about marriage and family living.

Sometimes when the counseling moves along well, such a statement as this will come up: "I have something to tell you, but I don't know how to start." Then the counselor will need to ascertain whether this is something to be said in the presence of the other member of the coupleship. If it is something to be said in private, then the arrangement should be made so that there will be no dwelling on a "secret sin" or "special weakness." Such a declaration may come early in the interviews or it may come late.

Sometimes the person wants to be relieved through early conversation since what he has to divulge may have bearing on the rest of the interviewing. One young man wanted the counselor to know that he was born "out of wedlock." This had bothered him in many ways and was blocking him in some of his approaches to marriage. The counselor caught the significance right away and did not raise an eyebrow. This item and the attending attitudes opened the way for many things that followed. It brought release to the groom-to-be.

This first interview, as are others, must be measured in length. An hour to an hour and a half would be a good time-length. The interview will close when the ground is well laid and the way ahead is outlined. There should be enough ground laid for asking the counselees what they would like to have discussed. This may need to be expanded and reinterpreted but it provides a starting point. The conference must be rounded out and terminated and not just closed off with a "Time's up!"

Generally by the close of the interview an atmosphere is created suitable to pastoral praying. This will add the spirit of including God in the conference as a guiding, interested member. This can open the way for insights into family worship. Something like this may express the tenor and the theme of the prayer. This is to be taken as indicative rather than as a prayer to be repeated.

> "Eternal Father, unto thee come Frank and Jane to find guidance, to receive instruction in taking a step of great moment to them and to all whose lives will touch theirs.
>
> "Together, Father, we are endeavoring to understand the stewardship of joining in marital companionship and of developing a home. We are trying to come with mind open to things as they are that we may lead with thy help into things that yet shall be.

We are wanting to see more clearly how they may walk together with thee. Help us, therefore, to see ourselves clearly, to see our relationships more understandingly, to be more responsive to thee, that thereby we may direct our way in accordance with thy plan and purpose for us all.

"Bless this son and daughter of thine that they may order their lives and build their home so they shall fit their family life into thy church as a household of faith and further the family potential in all mankind.

"We sense thy concern that these two shall come to marriage and into family living with enlightened common consent, with mutual regard for one another, and with consciousness of thy redeeming love.

"Bless Frank and Jane in their conversations, their explorations, their devotions today and till we meet again that they may find community of wholesome association.

"We want to confer together in the spirit of Jesus Christ that he may be with us in our wedding day as he was in the marriage in Cana of Galilee. Endow us richly with the light and love that were in him. Amen."

THE MINISTRY OF COUNSELING

The minister is a shepherd who wants to guide his sheep aright. He cannot accomplish his purpose by "going along." There are tremendous social currents and inherited factors. He will seek the resources of whatever associations and agencies have something to contribute. Sometimes he will discover that some proposed marriages ought not take place and that some that have taken place should not continue. He will need gifts of discernment in detecting factors for diagnoses and solutions. It is a tremendous responsibility to tamper with lives. Humbly he will seek to equip himself for counseling and will endeavor to draw on divine resources. Wisely he will utilize available disciplines of learning and will add that any diagnosis, any remedial program is incomplete if God is left out. In time he can say with Charles W. Stewart these concluding words in *The Minister as Marriage Counselor,*

"The counseling minister may never build a cathedral, but if he has helped one couple to find their moorings and to work through misunderstandings to acceptance of themselves under God, he may close the door of his study feeling a little more a pastor to his people and a shepherd of God."

ARRANGING FOR THE WEDDING

Marriage should be performed in a public religious service. Wherever possible the church sanctuary ought to be used for this purpose. The following suggestions are not arbitrary but are offered for the purpose of enhancing the marriage ceremony.

The use of the church building for any wedding is of course at the discretion of the administrative officers in charge, since they are responsible to see that such weddings as take place in the church harmonize with the basic teachings of the church concerning marriage. Arrangements for the use of the church should be made through the presiding elder of the congregation. Sunday weddings should be arranged with the presiding elder well in advance so as not to conflict with regular or specially arranged services of branch life.

The church sanctuary is available to members of the church as a part of the ministry of the church to them. It may be well to keep in mind that there are two classifications of weddings in churches. One uses the sanctuary only and no social or reception is involved. The other makes extensive preparations for a reception. In the second, the church should not be expected to assume the obligation. The engaging parties will be expected to care for the expense of such preparation and additional cost of maintenance. The church should not be denied to worthy nonmembers. Such wedding services, however, should be in harmony with the spirit and message of the church. As with members, arrangements for the use of the church should be made through the presiding elder of the congregation.

The church is to be respected at all times as the house of God. The throwing of rice and confetti in or around the church should be discouraged as it is not conducive to Christian worship. The throwing of more offensive or dangerous objects, such as old shoes, etc., should be prohibited. The use of tobacco is not permitted in any part of the building. If persons attend rehearsals or services while intoxicated or smelling offensively of liquor, they should be kindly asked to leave.

Decorations including floral installations should be appropriate and modest. Elaborate and ornate decorations are discouraged. Simplicity with minimum expense in harmony with good taste will always be desirable. The presiding elder, or in his absence the deacon in charge, may rule out any inappropriate decoration. White carpeting down the aisle may be used but is not necessary.

The regular deacon in charge of the congregation or someone else duly assigned shall be present at all rehearsals and should supervise the ushering at the service. Wedding ushers shall dress and deport themselves according to our standards of church ushering.

No pictures whatsoever should be taken during the ceremony nor even during the entering of the bridal party. The wedding party may return to the chapel afterward to pose for pictures.

When a reception is desired and the kitchen and social hall are to be used by members or friends of the church, the following suggestions will be helpful. When any group such as the women's circle quotes a price for the service rendered at the reception, it should include a reasonable fee agreed upon by the presiding elder and custodian for the proper cleaning of the church following the wedding. If profes-sional caterers are used a regular fee should be added for cleaning. If the family plan on doing their own cleaning, a cause of many problems, this should be worked out in cooperation with the presiding elder and the custodian. Some responsible person duly assigned should supervise the use and cleaning of the kitchen.

Interviews should be held with the minister on the meaning of Christian marriage. This will involve appointments in addition to the preliminary interview and rehearsal. Instructions are available in this manual.

Rehearsals are usually necessary and they will be held at a time agreeable to the minister and participants. In order to free the church for other activities on the same evening, rehearsal should be held punctually and, if possible, limited to one hour. The contracting parties will be responsible for the attendance of all participants. The officiating minister should be the director of the rehearsal. He will on some points ask for suggestions from the party and arrange for whatever special plans are appropriate. The deacon in charge or someone else assigned in his stead should be present at the rehearsal.

There are questions of procedure and of propriety. The following suggestions on etiquette and form are presented, with the realization that there is not just one way to direct the wedding service. We are sure that all of the principal points herein should become a part of all services with modifications in harmony with individual taste:

1. Cost involved. Inexpensive weddings are advisable under all circumstances. All weddings should be directed to the church when possible for both the poor and the rich. Those with means should not persist in putting on a lavish show. Such practice may direct comparison with those who cannot afford an elaborate wedding or cause some to obligate themselves beyond their means. The couple's friends will admire and approve moderation. They will criticize lavishness which is in poor taste and is poor

stewardship. Let the minister advise on decoration.

2. Ushers and Attendants. We have already said that the deacon in charge of the church should supervise the ushering. However, the candidates may select their close friends to usher and become a part of the wedding party and attendants. The minister should see that the candidates and attendants are made aware of the standards of the church as contained in this manual.

3. Ministers who may officiate. Any member of the Melchisedec priesthood or a priest of the Aaronic order in good standing in the church is authorized by the church to perform marriage ceremonies. (In some countries, including Canada, and in some states of the Union, a special license issued by the province or state is necessary.) A minister of the church who is requested to perform a marriage should immediately contact his presiding elder who will assist him and give valuable aid in arranging an impressive service.

4. Dress and makeup. The minister should advise all taking part in the wedding service to remember that this is the house of the Lord. He should see that startling costumes or immodest attire are avoided. Heavy makeup is in poor taste in church.

5. The wedding at the church (a suggested order of service):

> A. The ushers should arrive about one hour before the time for the ceremony. The deacon in charge will already have the church open. An usher will offer his right arm to the woman in each arriving party, escorting her down the aisle to her pew. Male attendants and children in each party follow. The front pews are reserved for the family and relatives. Parents of the groom sit in the first pew on the right. Parents of the bride sit in the first pew on the left. Relatives are to sit behind

respective families. In case of large weddings it may be advisable to reserve seats for the close relatives. After the relatives are seated, the candles if used are lighted. On the appointed hour the doors are closed. The groom's mother is then escorted to her seat by the usher. It is proper for the father to follow behind and take the seat by the side of his wife. The bride's mother is then escorted to her seat by the usher.

B.   Music and song. The organist, soloist, or choir enter in advance of the scheduled hour.

    (1) The organist begins the prelude from 15 to 30 minutes prior to the scheduled hour.

    (2) The choir is a lovely addition to a wedding and its use should be encouraged. The choir may be used instead of or in addition to the soloist. These musicians should enter just preceding the lighting of the candles, if candles are used. It is also in order for the congregation to sing a hymn.

C.   The wedding party.

    (1) The groom, the best man, and the minister wait in the vestry or study.

    (2) A white runner is neither recommended nor necessary, but if one is used, it is to be unrolled after the mothers have been ushered to their places.

    (3) The organist plays suitable prelude music during these arrangements.

    (4) The choir or soloist may then sing one or two numbers as desired or each may sing one number or the congregation may sing

an appropriate wedding hymn.

(5) The organ then plays for the processional of the minister, groom, and his best man. The other male attendants may enter with the groom and best man or they may come down the aisle and take their places after the groom has entered.

(6) Simultaneously the bride's procession commences, in the following order:

    (a) The bridesmaids may either take their places by coming down the aisle or may proceed about eight paces apart single file with the maid or matron of honor last.

    (b) The flower girl and ring bearer, if any, enter.

    (c) Then enters the bride on her father's right arm with a reasonable space between them and the persons immediately preceding them in the procession.

(7) The groom goes to meet the bride. He slips her right hand through his left arm. Usually they stand at the foot of the stairs facing the chancel.

    (a) The organ music stops.

    (b) The father has remained where the bride left him, on her left and a step or two behind her.

    (c) The minister usually asks, "Who gives this woman in marriage?" or "Who presents this woman for marriage?" The father then says, "I do," or "Her mother and I," or some appropriate remark such as this. The father then takes his seat beside his wife. (This whole step is not a requirement and some omit this act.)

(d) The soloist or choir may again sing, if desired, preceding the administration of the vows. The bride and groom take their places in front of the altar, and the bride hands her bouquet to the maid of honor. The minister faces the congregation; the bride is on the groom's left arm; both are facing the minister. The other attendants may be arranged as desired, the women on the side of the bride and the men on the side of the groom.

After the bride's father has been seated and the soloist or choir has sung, the minister then gives the prefatory address to the congregation and to the couple, impressing upon them the sacredness of the marriage rites and of the obligation devolving upon the contracting parties.

Following this prefatory statement it is proper to have a prayer with the couple either standing or kneeling, as desired by them. (The laying on of hands and the Lord's Supper are not a part of the rite of marriage.)

(e) After the vows are exchanged, and the pronouncement, the bride and groom may salute each other with a kiss. For this act the groom may turn back the veil. The maid of honor then returns the bride's bouquet.

(8) The bride, with her bouquet in her right hand, places her left hand on the groom's right arm. The recessional is played and the procession goes out in reverse order—the bride and groom first, followed by the maid of honor and the bridesmaids on the right arms of the best man and male attendants.

(9) The minister may then pronounce a short benediction on the service, if none has been included in the ceremony.

(10) Ushers return to escort the people from the church.

   (a) The bride's parents always are escorted out first.

   (b) The groom's parents follow next.

(11) Ushers finish escorting the people from the church.

   (a) All of the immediate families are next.

   (b) All of the rest of the guests leave from the front to the rear of the church.

D. The reception

(1) When the marriage takes place in a church and there is no reception following, the bride and groom may wait after the recessional in the narthex or entry of the church to receive the good wishes of the congregation.

(2) When there is a reception in the church parlors it is usually a good plan to proceed there immediately following the

recessional and form a receiving line at the beginning of the social hour.

(3) By previous arrangement someone will be hostess at the reception and a varied program may follow with refreshments and musical numbers.

E. In some countries it will be necessary for the couple to sign the marriage certificate prior to the pronouncement of their wedded state. The proper time to do this is after the pronouncement of all vows and just before they are pronounced husband and wife. The minister should be familiar with all legal requirements of the state in which he officiates.

The church has no set form for a marriage ceremony except the requirement that the "joint vow" as contained in Section 111 of the Doctrine and Covenants shall be used verbatim in all marriages performed in this church. The following service is suggested as a guide only. Each minister is advised to prepare ceremonies which may be amended to fit particular needs.

A SUGGESTED WEDDING CEREMONY

PRELUDE (See the chapter on "Planning Your Wedding Service" for appropriate music) Mothers to be ushered to their places

INVITATION TO WORSHIP

HYMN

"O Lord, Around Thine Altar Now" (*The Hymnal*, No. 42)—Solo or Congregation (See the chapter on "Planning Your Wedding Service" for other suggestions)

INVOCATION

STATEMENT OF BELIEFS ON MARRIAGE

SOLO

PROCESSIONAL (See chapter on "Planning Your Wedding Service" for appropriate music)

Appropriate Remarks by Minister: (such as)

On this happy occasion I am authorized to join ___________ and ___________ in the sacred bonds of marriage. In recognition that this ordinance is a provision of our heavenly Father and something more than a legal ceremony we ask you now to bow your heads in prayer.

(Prayer)

THE CHARGE

___________ and ___________, you come now before God and these witnesses to be joined in marriage. It is fitting that we reflect for a few moments on the meaning of this occasion.

Marriage is ideally a sacrament. At the heart of this sacrament is a covenant which you make with each other, and which you make together with God. This is a holy occasion, being a sacramental one, for some aspects of the will of God are revealed for your benefit, and your hearts shall be warmed and welded by the power of his Spirit. He is willing, if love is present, to honor marriage by his presence, even as his Son graced the wedding at Cana.

You recognize that life for each of you will be incomplete without the other. You have declared your devotion for each other. Now, with mingled feelings of joy and soberness you undergird your expressed affection with promises of fidelity and allegiance. In spite of untoward circumstances each will sustain the other. Joy shall be a mutual experience. Sorrow, too, is to be shared. This occasion is a pledge of mutually accepted responsibility.

Even as you pledge your fealty to each other, a promise is made by our heavenly Father. He will sustain you through the years with joy, and with strength for hours of sadness. Strive to merit the matchless gift of the Spirit of God. Let it be your mutual purpose to establish his cause in your hearts, in your home, and wherever you may labor.

Remember that the principles of the gospel are guarantees of wedded joy. Faith in God and in each other is the foundation of happiness. The spirit of repentance will help you to forsake self-justification, and, keeping you humble, will open your eyes to the needs and heartaches of the other. Perhaps there is no other single quality which smooths the pathway of adjustment as the spirit of repentance does. To be immersed in accomplishing God's purposes brings significance to individual life and even more profoundly to family life. To receive the influence of the Holy Spirit as an abiding comforter guarantees that you may constantly rise together in newness of life and understanding. You are admonished to base your married life on eternal values, and to exercise judgment and wisdom in your experience together.

While this is your marriage, it also belongs to God. We would remind you of the supreme value of prayer in the home. Add the activity of prayer to your own freedom of conversation with each other and you have an unbeatable combination toward understanding and lack of tension.

Cultivate the graciousness of a healthy sense of humor that you may smile at yourself, and with each other.

Find occasions for recreational expression which shall be at once creative and relaxing. The values of carefree association during the courtship need to be recaptured frequently to leaven and lighten the days of responsibility.

Let tenderness and patience abound, remembering the counsel of the apostle Paul concerning love:

"Love is patient and kind; love is not jealous or boastful; it is not arrogant or rude. Love does not insist on its own way; it is not irritable or resentful; it does not rejoice at wrong, but rejoices in the right. Love bears all things, believes all things, hopes all things, endures all things. Love never ends. . . . Faith, hope, love abide, these three; but the greatest of these is love."

THE MINISTER SHALL SAY:

[Groom's name], it is the privilege and duty of the husband to be the companion, counselor, and protector of his wife, shielding and caring for her, and heeding the divine command that a husband should love his wife as Christ loved the church and gave himself for it. Let your love be constantly revealed in thoughtful consideration, always qualifying your wishes and will by your concern for her welfare.

[Bride's name], the wife should be the faithful companion and solace of her husband, having for him an abiding affection, sharing with him life's problems as well as its joys, remembering the scriptural admonition that the ornament of a meek and quiet spirit is of great price in the sight of God.

THE WEDDING COVENANTS

[Groom's name], will you declare your wedding vow? (*or* [groom's name], please repeat after me) The groom shall say (*or* he shall repeat after the minister):

"[Bride's name], I take thee to be my wedded wife, to love and to cherish, to have and to hold, and forsaking all others, will cleave to thee and thee only so long as we both shall live."

The minister shall say:

[Bride's name], will you declare your wedding vow? (*or* [Bride's name], please repeat after me) The bride shall say (*or* she shall repeat after the minister):

"[Groom's name], I take thee to be my wedded husband, to love and to cherish, to have and to hold, and forsaking all others, will cleave to thee and thee only so long as we both shall live."

The minister shall say:

[Groom's name], do you have a ring? Place this token of your everlasting love upon the third finger of your bride's left hand and seal your marriage vows.

The groom shall place the ring on the bride's ring finger, saying:

"With this ring I seal our marriage vows."

The minister shall say (for double ring ceremonies):

[Bride's name], do you have a ring? Place this token of your everlasting love upon the third finger of your groom's left hand and seal your marriage vows.

The bride shall place the ring on the groom's ring finger, saying:

"With this ring I seal our marriage vows."
The minister shall say:

[Groom's name], [Bride's name]: *You both mutually agree to be each other's companion, husband and wife, observing the legal rights belonging to this condition; that is, keeping yourselves wholly for each other, and from all others, during your lives?*
The bride and groom shall reply, "Yes."

THE PRONOUNCEMENT

Then the minister shall continue:

Forasmuch as you have consented to live together in holy wedlock, and have witnessed the same before God and these friends, and thereto have pledged your faith to each other; therefore, in the name of the Lord Jesus Christ, and by virtue of the authority vested in me by the laws of this state, and of the church, I pronounce you husband and wife. *May God add his blessings and keep you to fulfill your covenants from henceforth and forever. Amen.* What God has joined together let no man put asunder.

THE BENEDICTION (Or a similar brief benediction)

Let us pray. Our heavenly Father, thou hast kindled in these hearts the fire of a divine love. Wilt thou keep it always aflame upon the altar of their souls. Wilt thou make their home a place of light and truth, a place of beauty, a place of joy and happiness all the days of their lives. In Jesus' name, amen.

SOLO: "Wedding Prayer" or other suitable benedictory music; see the chapter on "Planning Your Wedding Service."

PRESENTATION of Mr. and Mrs.________________________

RECESSIONAL: (See the next chapter, "Planning Your Wedding Service," for appropriate music.)

PLANNING YOUR WEDDING SERVIC

(This chapter is available in brochure form to
give to each engaged couple.)
By Franklyn S. Weddle

You want your wedding to be unforgettable, a memory
you will cherish together. It is to be a time of joy. It
deserves to be graced by dignity and a special kind of
beauty, the beauty of holiness. Your marriage can be
sacramental, as well as legal.

In some countries the wedding is a civil ceremony
performed by a magistrate or some other official of
government. There is no provision for a religious setting. In
such countries our church people go from the civil
ceremony to the church for a wedding service. They want
an extra quality to be added, recognizing that marriage is
divinely ordained and may be divinely guided and strengthened.

Perhaps in your nation ministers of the gospel are
permitted to perform weddings. A clergyman is authorized
by the state to solemnize marriages. The legal pronouncement of marriage becomes part of the religious ceremony
and the minister is expected to bolster each new home with
social, moral, and spiritual stability. The church is enabled
to encourage a couple to expand their covenant to include
commitment to Christ who lends unifying purpose and
spirit to the new family.

Whether your church ceremony follows after, or con-
tains the legal requirements, let it be the means of lifting
your wedding above the secular. Make it truly sacramental,
an ordinance and a worship experience.

Is the wedding a service of worship? It should be. It is,

when conducted in a place set apart for the worship of God. Here vows are made in the presence of God and "these witnesses," who are the congregation. The service moves from recognition and adoration of God to dedication for those who make their covenant and rededication by those who witness the covenant. All who are gathered are intent upon a decision in harmony with the will of God.

It is appropriate that the wedding service should recognize the centrality of our creator. The attention of all is to be drawn to him. Adoration of the bride and groom for each other, as important as this is, is enhanced as they together join in adoration of God. It is their most important uniting which sanctifies their union from this day forward.

In a wedding service it is easy for other things to take precedence, even detracting from the worship of God. The wedding gown, flowers, ringbearers, music—and even the manner in which the bride and groom conduct themselves—are all to be conducive to the experiencing of worship. To keep in mind that the wedding service which joins two persons is a joyful act of God-directed, Christ-centered worship will solve many of the usual questions and problems that seem to cluster around weddings.

Those who attend a church wedding should come as worshipers rather than as spectators. Each participant may share a sense of joy with the bride and groom. They will come to thank and to praise. They will come to pray for God's blessing upon the marriage. Strange as it may seem, the wedding service is not for the bride and groom alone but for all who attend.

It is right to share the service as a congregation of worshipers. The presence of the congregation is a reminder that the new family is part of a larger family, interested and ready to encourage the successful development of a new home. There are obligations both ways.

It is our belief that the marriage rite is a public act of the church, subject to the public ministry of the church. The church, therefore, has a responsibility to see that the ordinance of marriage is carried out in a reverent, dignified manner, in harmony with the law of the church and the intent of the heavenly Father who instituted marriage. The minister is expected to see that the ordinance is conducted in harmony with the principles of the church's worship.

A couple uniting in marriage need every good resource toward a successful life together. It is good to know of the solid backing of Saints and friends when launching out in marriage. Congregational participation in the wedding service represents a resource of shared concern. Of course, there will be particular guests invited by the bride and the groom, but these, too, can share in the celebration as active participants in praise, thanksgiving, and dedication.

Every person attending the wedding can be involved in active participation so that there is a real sense of sharing in this happy and holy moment. Witnessing and sharing in the service should stimulate those already married to renew their vows and those who are approaching the step to consider carefully its implications. The children present are to be reminded that the marriage rite is instituted by God and that marriage is to be approached with care and prayer.

One of the best ways to realize the strength and support of the church at the time of the wedding is to emphasize the corporate congregational character of worship. This can be done by providing opportunity for active participation. Such involvement may be in responsive reading of scriptures and in music.

Music is an integral part of most church worship. Of course, it is possible to worship without music, but it would be unusual. It is difficult to think of the wedding service without music.

Music can be instrumental in promoting a joyful Christ-centered experience; or if unwisely chosen, music can be detrimental to worship. This is why it is necessary in choosing music for any worship service, including the wedding service, to read the words and ask this question: "Are the words such that the minister would find them appropriate to quote as a part of the wedding service?" If he would find them inappropriate, that music should not be used by a congregation, choir, or soloist. The selection of all music which goes into the wedding service should be made in consultation with the organist and minister, the final decision resting with the latter.

We mentioned involvement of the congregation through music. This may include congregational singing. In many places the tradition of congregational hymn singing at wedding services is practiced or is being revived. The singing of a hymn by the congregation can be an excellent way of helping all assembled to share in the thanks, praise, and invoking of God's blessings upon the marriage.

A well-chosen congregational hymn would be appropriate following the entrance of the bridal party, or immediately following the marriage rite, or at both times. The bride and groom should remember that they, too, are part of the worshiping congregation. As such, they should join in the singing of the hymns. They may do this from memory or by singing from a hymnal or printed order of service.

Hymns of trust, obedience, invocation, and the like are most appropriate. *The Hymnal* has a selection of wedding hymns as well as other more general hymns which are appropriate. The following will help to suggest suitable material:

"The King of Love My Shepherd"   No. 137
"The Lord's My Shepherd"   132

Other hymns will also suggest themselves with a careful look through *The Hymnal.*

In July 1950, during the intermission of a Sunday afternoon broadcast of the New York Philharmonic Orchestra, Richard Wagner's granddaughter was being interviewed when the subject of Wagner's second marriage came up. The interviewer, Mr. James Fassett, asked if the "Bridal Chorus" from *Lohengrin* and Mendelssohn's "Wedding March" from the music for *A Midsummer Night's Dream* were used at the wedding. Wagner's granddaughter replied, "Goodness no! We never heard of it in Europe until we saw it in the movies, and then we thought it was a Hollywood joke; besides I would be too superstitious to get married to the 'Bridal Chorus' . . . the marriage of Lohengrin and Elsa did not last long." She knew that the opera itself is a story of infidelity and separation. No wonder she felt the "Bridal Chorus" to be inappropriate for a service of Christian marriage.

Even if a wedding service has no other music it is almost certain to have music accompanying the entrance and recessional of the bridal party. If a processional hymn is not used, special processional music is usually played by the organist, and the recessional is almost always played by the organist. Music for the processional and recessional should reflect the same concerns for meaningful worship which we have already considered. In the church wedding, music for the processional and recessional does more than provide music for "going in" and "coming out"; it also offers an opportunity to share in the expression of worship.

Music based on hymns and chorales is always appropriate and useful. This especially is so when the processional is immediately followed by the singing of the same hymn on which it is based. The recessional may also be based on one of the hymns sung earlier in the service. The music for the processional and recessional should be consistent with the solemn, yet joyful, dignity of the wedding service and indeed the marriage itself.

There is a large body of music easily available and well suited for the kind of wedding service we describe. Some of it is listed under the music suggested in the closing pages of this booklet.

All music should be selected in consultation with the organist and minister to reflect the highest standards of worship. Here are some suggestions in planning music for the processional and recessional:

Precedent and custom are very severe taskmasters in the culture of our time. It takes a great deal of courage, *and conviction,* to break with custom even when we know in our hearts that we should do better than to follow its path. Do not ask your organist to use "old favorites" simply because everyone else chooses them. Many of them have no place in a church ordinance.

Avoid different or special music for the entrance of the bride. The procession of the entire bridal party is more effectively accomplished when one fitting selection is played for all. Do not attempt to "march" to the processional music. Simply *walk* slowly, with dignity and reverence. This music is a processional, not a *march*.

Undue haste should be avoided in the recessional—but it can appropriately move a bit more quickly than the processional.

Use organ music selected with the ability of the organist and organ in mind. Music which is fitting for the wedding service can be found readily available on every level of difficulty. The determining factor for suitability is not the difficulty of the music but rather its usefulness as a means of worship. On some occasions where adequate resources are available, music of a more elaborate nature may be appropriately used.

The choir may be used in a church wedding service as well as in other services of the church. Hymns or suitable anthems may be used. The choir should be an integral part of the worship of the wedding service and not just an added "attraction." The use of vocal solos in the wedding service is a practice well established and is usually more easily arranged than the participation of a choir. Many of the hymns suitable for choir or congregational singing may also be sung as solos. Much care must be used in choosing both the soloist and the solo to be used. Much of the material frequently heard at weddings is far removed from God-directed, Christ-centered worship.

Most of the solos which are traditionally used are secular in character, both in words and music. They lack the dignity, reverence, and sincerity of expression suitable to a marriage service and are preoccupied with secular love rather than sacred love. A list of solo material is appended to the end of this chapter.

Frequently the soloist is called upon to sing a musical

setting of the "Lord's Prayer." The most well-known of these settings is more theatrical than worshipful and is more in the mood of a concert setting than a worship setting. Since the wedding service is a corporate, congregational service it is more appropriate to use the "Lord's Prayer" offered in unison by the entire congregation or by the minister at an appropriate place in the service.

There is no dearth of suitable music; we need only to exercise care and judgment in its selection and performance.

INSTRUMENTAL MUSIC

The violin, flute, or oboe can be used very effectively in the wedding service if they are properly employed. Groups of instruments may be used with the organ to reflect the varying moods of the service. They are particularly effective when used in a preservice prelude. If, however, such music cannot be carefully selected and performed it is best omitted.

IN CONCLUSION

The dignity of the sanctuary and the deep significance of the service are basic guides for planning for music in the church service, whatever the occasion.

For the wedding service, and during the time for the congregation and friends to assemble, the music may reflect moods lofty and serious, joyful and festive—all with the underlying thought of centering our worship in Christ and directing it to God, our heavenly Father. The trivial and frivolous have no place here, nor have the popular favorites which excel in recalling and emphasizing secular, social, or sentimental personal associations.

During the ceremony music should not be interpolated just for the sake of having music for entertainment, nor is background music on the organ during prayers, ceremony, or readings desirable or in good taste.

Music after the rite of marriage, including the recessional, is appropriately joyful, yet dignified.

Music for the reception—a social occasion—may be drawn from the more intimate or subjective works of fine composers. Here it may be possible to comply with request numbers that stay within the bounds of propriety and good taste.

What we have suggested here will be different from what you have experienced in "traditional weddings." This is because the traditional has not always been thought of in terms of worship. And yet, we observe on every hand the need to deepen the sacramental significance of marriage. Persons of conviction and courage will be willing to venture.

It may not be easy for immediate families and friends to assimilate the views we have shared in this discussion. They may never have questioned the propriety of using secular or theatrical materials in a worship setting. Perhaps we can help by placing in the hands of each one attending the service a small leaflet which includes a welcome statement, an order of service, and a statement of the belief of the church regarding marriage.

The statement of welcome could be something like this:

"You have been invited to share in a happy and holy occasion—the wedding service. This is a service of worship in which a covenant is established between husband and wife in the presence of God. You are present to join, always inwardly and sometimes audibly, in this act of worship. Perhaps you are already married. For you this may be a time of remembrance and renewal of vows. Perhaps you are contemplating marriage. Then join with us in this place of prayer, where we shall all be reminded that marriage is divinely ordained and is to be kept sacred through joy and adversity.

"This is an hour of worship, dedicated to God. The presence of his Spirit during this service depends in part upon your preparation and participation. As you wait, we invite you to meditate and pray, letting these words call you to worship:

"Know ye that the Lord he is God;
It is he that hath made us,
And not we ourselves;
We are his people,
And the sheep of his pasture.
Enter into his gates with thanksgiving,
And into his courts with praise;
Be thankful unto him,
And bless his name.
For the Lord is good;
His mercy is everlasting;
And his truth endureth to all
        generations."

—Psalm 100:3-5.

Your minister has additional resources available to help you in planning your wedding. Orders of worship, a more complete listing of music, wedding etiquette, and procedures for counseling are outlined for him in *A Marriage Manual for Ministers*. You are invited to participate in counseling interviews in preparation for your life together. Your minister will help in general counsel and in specific preparation of the wedding service. He has been advised to direct you to professional counselors for advice concerning your physical adjustments. Your church stands by to assist you as you work out relationships with each other.

We join you in the desire for an unforgettable wedding— and a memorable marriage.

A STATEMENT OF BELIEF

We believe that marriage is within the divine purpose.

We believe that marriage is sacramental, and should be solemnized worshipfully by a minister of appropriate authority according to the legal requirements of the state.

We believe that marriage unites a man and a woman in mutual obligation and joy, and that such an agreement should be entered into thoughtfully and prayerfully, with sincerity and humility.

We believe that marriage involves a stewardship for each, and that husband and wife are to live in harmony with the will of God as it concerns the family and the home.

We believe that marriage is a covenant to bring forth children and to rear them in reverence which is the cornerstone of the Christian home.

MUSIC FOR YOUR WEDDING

Organ Music Preceding the Wedding Service

Bach, J. S.

"Air in D" (arr. *Whitney*)   G. Schirmer

Aria, "When Thou Art Near"
(Wedding Music for the Organ)   Flammer

"Arioso"   G. Schirmer

"Prelude in D" (arr. *Guilmant*)   Durand

"Prelude in G" (Wedding Music
Vol. I)   Concordia

Boellmann, L.

"Priere a' Notre Dame" (Wedding
Music Vol. I)   Concordia

Handel, G. F.

"Larghetto," from Concerto (Wedding
Music for the Organ)   Flammer

Karg-Elert, S.
  "Rejoice Greatly O My Soul" (Service
    Music for Organ)   J. Fischer
Liszt, F.
  "Adagio" (Useful Service Music for
    Organ)   Wood
Peeters, F.
  "Aria"   Heuwekemeijer
                                        (Holland)

Williams, R. V.
  "Rhosymedre" (Three Preludes)   Stainer & Bell
                                        (Galaxy)

Wright, S.
  Prelude on "Brother James's Air"   Oxford

Processionals

Bach, J. S.
  "Adagio in A Minor" (Wedding
    Music Vol. I)   Concordia
  "Sinfonia to Wedding Cantata,"
    No. 196 (Porter)   H. W. Gray

Boellmann, L.
  "Choral" (Suite Gothique) (Wedding
    Music Vol. I)   Concordia

Campre, A.
  "Rigaudon" (A Treasury of Shorter
    Organ Classics, ed. Biggs)   Mercury

Ganne, L.
  "March Nuptiale" (Standard
    Organ Pieces)   D. Appleton Century

Handel, G. F.
  "Aria from Concerto Grosso XII"
    (Wedding Music Vol. I)   Concordia
  "Processional in G Major"
    (Wedding Music Vol. I)   Concordia
Marcello, B.
  "Psalm XIX"
    (Wedding Music Vol. I)   Concordia
  "Psalm XX"
    (Wedding Music Vol. I)   Concordia
Purcell, H.
  "Largo in D Major" (Purcell to
    Handel, ed. Nevins)   H. W. Gray
  "March in C" (A Second Book
    of Wedding Pieces)   Oxford
Walther, J. G.
  "Lord Jesus Christ, Be Present Now"
    (Wedding Music Vol. II)   Concordia

Recessionals

Dunstable, J.
  "Agincourt Hymn" (Treasury of Early
    Organ Music, ed. Biggs)   Mercury
Eldridge, G. H.
  "Fanfare" (Fanfares and Processionals
    for Organ)   Novello
Goss, J.
  "Praise, My Soul, the King of Heaven"
    (Wedding Music for the Church
    Organist and Soloist, ed.
    Lovelace)   Abingdon
Handel, G. F.
  "Postlude in G Major" (Wedding
    Music Vol. I)   Concordia

Jacob, G.
   "Festal Flourish" (An Album of
      Praise)   Oxford
Karg-Elert, S.
   "Now Thank We All Our God"   Marks
Purcell, H.
   "Trumpet Tune in C" (A Second
      Book of Wedding Pieces)   Oxford
   "Trumpet Tune in D Major"
      (Wedding Music Vol. I)   Concordia
   "Trumpet Voluntary in D Major"
      (Wedding Music Vol. I)   Concordia
Saxton, S. E.
   "Fanfare and Tuba Tune"   Galaxy
Wesley, S. S.
   "Choral Song" (Wedding Music
      Vol. I)   Concordia

Vocal Music

Bach, J. S.
   "Jesus Shepherd, Be Thou Near
      Me"   Concordia
   "Jesus, Lead Our Footsteps Ever"
      (Whittaker)   Oxford University Press
   "Like a Shepherd, God Doth Guide
      Us"   Concordia
   "Jesu, Joy of Man's Desiring"   Concordia
   "Trust in the Lord," Cantata 174
      (Diack)   Concordia
   "My Heart Ever Faithful"   G. Schirmer
Bach-Dickinson
   "God, My Shepherd"   H. W. Gray

Bach-Fryxell
   "Praise, My Soul, the King of
      Heaven"   Augustana Book Concern
Bairstow
   "The King of Love My Shepherd
      Is"   Oxford University Press
Bitgood, R.
   "The Greatest of These Is Love"   H. W. Gray

Brahms, J.
   "Though I Speak with the Tongues"
     (Four Serious Songs)   Carl Fischer
Bunjes, Paul (Ed.)
   "Wedding Blessings" (SC 18)   Concordia
   "Wedding Blessings" (SC 19)   Concordia
Burleigh, H. T.
   "O Perfect Love"   Theodore Presser

Cassler, G. Winston
   "Whither Thou Goest"   Augsburg Publishing House

Charles, Ernest
   "Love Is of God"   G. Schirmer
Clokey, Jos.
   "O Perfect Love" (Wedding
     Suite)   J. Fischer & Bro.
   "Set Me as a Seal upon Thine Heart"
     (Wedding Suite)   J. Fischer & Bro.
Davies, Ivor
   "May the Grace of Christ, Our Savior"   Novello & Co.

Diggle, Ronald
   "A Wedding Prayer"   G. Schirmer
Dunlap, Fern Glasglow
   "Wedding Prayer"   G. Schirmer

Dvorak, Anton
"God Is My Shepherd" (Vol. I)
Associated Music Pub.
"I Will Sing New Songs of Gladness"
(Vol. I)   Associated Music Pub.
Fetler, David
"O Father, All Creating"   Concordia
Franck, Cesar
"O Lord Most Holy"   G. Schirmer
Fryxell, Regina H.
"Psalm 67"   H. W. Gray
"Praise to the Lord" (S.A.T.B.
or solo)   H. W. Gray
"O Come, Creator Spirit, Come"
(S.A.T.B. or solo)   Augustana Book Concern

"The Lord's Prayer" (S.A.T.B., unison
or solo)   Augustana Book Concern
Gore, R.
"O Perfect Love"   Augustana Book Concern

Gounod
"Entreat Me Not to Leave Thee"   Oliver Ditson Co.

Holst
"The Heart Worships"   Galaxy Music Corp.

Hummel
"Hallelujah" (Alleluia)   Ricordi
Jacob
"Brother James's Air" (Solo or unison,
arr. *Trew*)   Oxford University Press
Lang, C. S.
"Hail, Gladdening Light" (Evening—
Unison)   Novello

Ley
 "The Lord's Prayer" (Unison) Oxford University Press

Liddle, Samuel
 "The Lord Is My Shepherd" Boosey & Hawkes

Lloyd, Henry
 "O Christ, Who Once Hast Deigned" Concordia

Lovelace, Austin
 "A Wedding Benediction" G. Schirmer
 "A Wedding Blessing" G. Schirmer
 "We Lift Our Hearts to Thee" Concordia
MacDermid
 "Ninety-first Psalm" Forster

Markworth, Henry
 "Oh, Blest the House Whate'er
  Befall" (Duet) Concordia
Mendelssohn, F.
 "If With All Your Hearts" G. Schirmer
 "The Voice That Breathed o'er
  Eden" Concordia
O'Connor—Morris
 "The Lord Is My Shepherd" Carl Fischer
Polack, H. A.
 "The Lord Be With You" Concordia
 "Wedding Song" Concordia
Roberts
 "If With All Your Hearts" Theo. Presser
Rowley, A.
 "Here at Thine Altar, Lord"
  (S.A.T.B. or solo) Novello & Co.
Schuetz, Heinrich
 "Wedding Song" (high—Lenel)
  (low—Leupold) Chantry Music Press

Sowerby, Leo
   "O Perfect Love"   H. W. Gray
Thiman
   "The God of Love My Shepherd Is"   Novello & Co.
   "Thou Wilt Keep Him In Perfect
      Peace"   H. W. Gray
Watts, Wintter
   "Entreat Me Not to Leave Thee"   G. Schirmer

Weaver, Powell
   "Build Thee More Stately
      Mansions"   Galaxy
Willan, Healey
   "O Perfect Love"   H. W. Gray
   "Eternal Love" (Three Songs of
      Devotion)   C. C. Birchard & Co.
Vaughan Williams, R.
   "O How Amiable" (Mixed
      Voices, 2 parts, or solo)   Oxford University Press

Young, Gordon
   "Entreat Me Not to Leave Thee"   Galaxy

A CHECKLIST FOR PLANNING
YOUR WEDDING SERVICE

Have you . . .

1. Arranged for consultations with the officiating minister?
2. Obtained the premarital counseling brochure *So You're Getting Married . . . ?*
3. Secured approval of date and time for the use of the church in which your wedding service is to be held?
4. Consulted with your organist?

5. Made arrangements with soloist or choral group?
6. Made arrangements with the church custodian for rehearsal, wedding, and/or reception needs?
7. Selected florist, if floral arrangements are included?
8. Selected and consulted with photographer?
9. Made plans for reception?
10. Complied with civil requirements of securing your marriage license? (Give license to minister at rehearsal)
11. Arranged for dressing and transportation details for the wedding party?

Dates and other information to remember:
1. Dates for consultations with minister _______________
2. Date of Wedding _______________
   Time _______________
3. Date of rehearsal _______________
   Time _______________
4. Participants in wedding (in addition to principals)
   maid of honor _______________
   bridesmaids _______________

   ____

   ____

   ____

   groomsmen _______________

   ____

   ____

   ____

   flower girl _______________
   ring bearer _______________

ushers _______________________________________

____

____

guest book _______________________________________
reception assistants _______________________________________

____

5. Music selected for
   processional _______________________________________

   recessional _______________________________________

   hymns by the congregation _______________________________________

   ____

   ____

   solo or choral numbers _______________________________________

   ____

   ____

   ____

APPENDIX A

WORLD CONFERENCE RESOLUTIONS RE MARRIAGE AND FAMILY LIFE

No. 272—Adopted April 9, 1884.

Whereas, We believe that marriage is ordained of God, and that the law of God provides for but one companion in wedlock, for either man or woman—except in cases where the contract is broken by death or transgression; therefore

Resolved, That it is our understanding that in case of separation of husband and wife, one of which is guilty of the crime of fornication, or adultery, the other becomes released from the marriage bond, and if they so desire may obtain a divorce and marry again.

No. 872—Adopted April 7, 1927.

Resolved, That:

1. Inasmuch as the need of the day is the establishment of Zionic homes, and as this task concerns both men and women, the departments cooperate in the formation of parent classes for the study of parent problems. Further, that these classes be conducted at an hour when it is possible for the babies to be in the care of a trained nursery mother, preferably at the church school hour; that whenever available trained teachers conduct these classes, and that institute work be provided for the training of other parent-teachers.

2. Believing it advisable to enlarge the scope of the Cradle Roll to insure the entrance of children into the public schools with healthy bodies and normal mental development through the use of baby clinics and nurseries and by means of parent instruction, the name "Cradle

Roll" be changed to "Pre-School Age."

3. As the program of religious education adopted by the church includes not only pulpit instruction but also classwork and expressional activity for all ages, new church buildings provide such facilities as parlors, kitchens, reading rooms, and nurseries.

4. Since each leader of the departments of religious education, pastor, missionary, church school superintendent, recreation and expression leader, and superintendent of the Department of Women, working alone, to a degree defeats the purpose of the church, these forces work as a council in each branch, analyze the needs of its membership, and supply those needs in which every department or combination of departments can best meet such needs. Thus classwork, expressional activity, and sermon may all combine to inculcate definite Zionic principles, such as the gospel of good health, stewardship, economic soundness in family life, wholesome recreation, the Sunday program, etc.

No. 972—Adopted April 8, 1950.

One of the most important contributions we can make to the establishment of the kingdom is in the refinement of our home and family life. True marriage is a sacrament, and should not be entered into lightly, hastily, or unworthily. In particular, members of the church should not enter into this covenant relationship with persons who do not realize its sacramental nature, or who do not feel deeply their spiritual obligation to abide by its sacrificial demands, as well as to enjoy its happy rewards. Pastors and other ministers of mature judgment will do well to teach these things to our young people before they are called on to choose their life partners. And an ever greater responsibility is carried by Latter Day Saint parents, whose example will go so far to determine the quality and durability of the homes of tomorrow. Let the church be admonished that the kingdom is now seeking expression in the homes of the faithful, and that far more significant for the kingdom, than any material resources we may bring, are such spiritual qualities as industry, forethought, thrift, cooperation, kindness, temperance, patience, and compassion which are best matured in saintly homes.

When divisive forces are already found at work in church families, we suggest most soberly that the Saints who are involved seek out their pastors or other ministers of mature judgment and secure their help in effecting reconciliation before these differences become unsupportable. And ministers who are asked to advise in such delicate situations should take particular care to prove themselves both compassionate and trustworthy. Failure to seek and to give such ministry as is here suggested means that in far too many cases the first official contact of the church with divided homes and with children threatened by the worst kind of insecurity is when someone suggests that punitive measures should be applied.

No. 1034—Adopted April 6, 1962.

1. Marriage is ordained of God: "Marriage is ordained of God unto man" (Doctrine and Covenants 49:3a)

2. Divinely approved purposes of marriage are mutual companionship, pro-creation within families, and mutual fulfillment: "It is lawful that he should have one wife, and they twain shall be one flesh, and all this that the earth might answer the end of its creation; and that it might be filled with the measure of man, according to his creation before the world was made" (Doctrine and Covenants 49:3; see also Genesis 2:27-30; Ephesians 5:31; Doctrine and Covenants 111:2b).

3. Marriage is intended to be a lifelong covenant between one man and one woman. In the event of the death of

either spouse, the other is at liberty to marry again: "One man should have one wife; and one woman but one husband, except in case of death, when either is at liberty to marry again" (Doctrine and Covenants 111:4b; see also Matthew 19:5-8).

4. Marriage should be entered into soberly, worthily, and after mature consideration. Members of the church should marry only such persons as realize the sacramental nature of the marriage covenant and are willing to abide by its necessary conditions as well as to enjoy its rewards (see G.C.R. 972).

5. God is concerned in every marriage. Marriages should therefore be solemnized with dignity in a setting conducive to worship. To this end, simplicity, propriety, and frugality in the service and its appointments are advised. Civil marriages, though legally acceptable, recognize only the civil significance of the compact and so tend to minimize the spiritual values involved. In order to preserve the sacramental nature of marriage in countries where civil marriages are required by law, a second ceremony is encouraged. This ceremony is to be conducted by authorized priesthood in the recommended worshipful setting.

6. Members of the Melchisedec priesthood or priests of the Aaronic order may solemnize marriages when so permitted by civil law (Doctrine and Covenants 111:1b, c). Officiating ministers should require that they be given sufficient time by the parties seeking their services to enable them to make such investigation and to give such instruction and counsel as they deem helpful in maintaining the sacramental nature of the marriage covenant and of the marriage itself.

7. The church recognizes that the remarriage of an innocent party in a divorce action is permissible when a divorce has been secured for any of the following reasons:

adultery, repeated sexual perversion, desertion, such aggravated conditions within the home as render married life unbearable for the party petitioning or for the children of the marriage.*

8. Though the civil court may have accepted proof of lesser indignities as sufficient grounds for divorce, permission for remarriage should be granted only when the conditions complained of were of such an extreme nature as to place the other members of the family in serious and continuing jeopardy.

Persons who have been divorced, even though innocent of wrongdoing, should pay special attention to the admonition not to marry hastily or without due consideration. Ministers asked to officiate at such weddings should assure themselves that sufficient time has elapsed and that due consideration has been had.

9. Any person who has been divorced, and who desires to be married by a member of the priesthood, should make arrangements with this minister in sufficient time to permit him to make any necessary inquiry concerning the circumstances of the divorce and to secure the approval of the branch president. If the branch president does not feel free to act, he should refer the inquiry to the next higher administrative officer of the church.

No. 1047—Adopted April 11, 1964
[Note especially the paragraph relating to the education of youth in matters of morality, ethics, and behavior and the one referring to premarital counseling.]

---

*This is in harmony with the basic requirements of the law and also takes note of the fact that circumstances develop and persist in certain marriages for which no remedy within that marriage seems to be discoverable, and which are so harmful in their effects on one or both of the partners to the marriage, and on their children, as to render life under those circumstances humiliating, fraught with suffering, and intolerable.

Whereas, The church has the unique mission of preparing for the establishment of Zion; and

Whereas, The accomplishment of this mission will require the development of a generation of church members who are equipped adequately with spiritual, moral, ethical, educational, and vocational resources to bring this monumental task to fruition; and

Whereas, The church has a consequent responsibility of assuming some leadership in making the land of America a suitable headquarters for God's kingdom on earth; and

Whereas, The decisions of the Supreme Court of the United States on religious observances in schools give further emphasis to the leadership which must be taken by the church to give young people a suitable sense of values and direction; and

Whereas, It is more desirable for young people to be guided and assisted by the church motivated by Christian principles than by paternalistic governments motivated by political considerations; now, therefore, be it

Resolved, That the World Church in Conference assembled does hereby request each appropriate department and quorum of the church and each congregation, district, and stake to give prayerful consideration and added emphasis in various aspects of the church programs to helping young people in and out of the church achieve the desire and skills to help build a perfect society under the kingship of Christ. Be it further

Resolved, That the curriculum of the church school be broadened to incorporate more emphasis on Christian morality, ethics, and behavior in addition to doctrine and church history. Be it further

Resolved, That appropriate World Church departments prepare specific recommendations, disseminate appropriate bibliographies to aid in self-preparation, and provide field training to local personnel to carry out programs to make

114

our churches outstanding and attractive focal points for practical ministry to young people, members and non-members alike. Specifically, there should be provided training in the fields of recreation, personal counseling including premarital counseling, and cooperation with available community services such as the family service and other professional helps.

Resolved, That local congregations be urged to mobilize all available resources and to provide local leadership for community efforts to (1) help young people locate suitable employment, (2) help young people complete worthy and practical educational objectives, (3) prevent school drop-outs prior to completion of high school, (4) provide skilled and needed counseling services, resorting to professional assistance outside the church when necessary, and (5) provide a sufficiently attractive program of wholesome recreation and social life that young people will be drawn to church-centered fellowship and thus seek what effective ministry the church is prepared to offer in other aspects of their lives.

Resolved, That in order to help overcome the reluctance of some to take advantage of available helps due to past convention and misunderstanding of the nature of counseling, that appropriate World Church departments strongly urge all young people by every practicable means available to make use of all available programs. Vocational, educational, and premarital counseling are cited for specific example and emphasis.

No. 1054—Adopted April 22, 1966.

Whereas, The responsibility of the church toward effective family life is to bring ministry of moral uplift and spiritual enlightenment to families and individuals, and to build strong family ties through consistent ministry in the home, and

Whereas, The present problems of divorce, family

disharmony, and emotional disturbance are evidences that our present program of family ministry is not providing a sufficiently strong resource to meet present needs, therefore, be it

Resolved, That we reaffirm that the basic ministerial responsibility for the spiritual and moral well-being of family life and the development of sound family relationships lies with the priesthood functioning in their several callings, and be it further

Resolved, That renewed emphasis be given to this important aspect of this distinctive ministry in the church by appointment of a Coordinator for Family Ministry for the World Church whose responsibility shall entail:

1. Working with the various departments of the church in the development of a long-range plan for family ministry and to supervise the development of a methodology with adequate materials and helps to achieve this purpose.
2. Working with stakes (and large districts when possible) in order to:
   a. Formulate a more effective program in preventative counseling leading toward stronger family relationships. This would include premarital counseling among our young people with a view toward the development of wholesome attitudes about marital life.
   b. Develop a better program of therapeutic counseling through the use of qualified personnel in the church and referral to those secular agencies which provide effective help.
3. Calling upon our membership who are engaged in related professional disciplines for advice, counsel, and evaluation of the program.
4. Reporting annually to the First Presidency with

consideration being given to the printing of these reports for benefit of and information to the church.

No. 1059—Adopted April 1, 1968.

Whereas, Assistance in the establishment of well-adjusted Christian families is among the great objectives of the church, therefore be it

Resolved, That the 1968 World Conference recognize that both in the church and in society there are many unmarried adults who would benefit from a ministry designed to assist them in establishing Christian, Zionic homes. To develop and implement specific and practical programs in this ministerial endeavor will require the efforts of skilled professionals and the use of modern technology. The Conference, therefore, refers this matter to the First Presidency with the suggestion that either the Committee on Ministry to Unmarried Adults continue to function and make further recommendations, or that this specialized ministry be included in the responsibility of the Family Ministry Coordinator.

No. 1066—Adopted April 5, 1968.

Whereas, The strength of the church is dependent upon the strength of the families which comprise its membership, and

Whereas, The emotional and interpersonal problems of our youth, our married couples, and our families continue to be apparent, and

Whereas, The 1966 World Conference resolved that renewed emphasis should be given to various specific aspects of an expanded program of family ministry, including educative, preventive, and restorative aspects, to be directed by a coordinator of family ministry, and

Whereas, A Coordinator of Family Ministry and a Family Ministry Advisory Committee have been appointed and are working and planning together, now, therefore, be it

Resolved, That the church move decisively into an expanded family ministry program by establishing a program budget of $30,000.00 for the 1968-69 biennium.

APPENDIX B

STANDING HIGH COUNCIL ACTIONS RE MARRIAGE AND FAMILY LIFE

I. Factors in Education for Marriage

The following factors are important in the church's program of education for marriage:

1. The church should teach her people of all ages that the marriage covenant should be for life, and that the home and family are the basic social units through which the cause of the kingdom of God is advanced.
2. This educational program should be graded to be in keeping with the *age* and *experience* range of a given class group.
3. Sex should not be introduced into this curriculum until the age group is ready for it. Sex is only part of the whole subject to be covered. Up to a point more emphasis should be placed on the religious, social, and other aspects of marriage and homelife.
4. Such teaching should be based on materials prepared by recognized authorities. When the course is in operation adequate teacher supervision should be given.
5. The priesthood of the church should teach, in the homes of the Saints, in classes, and from the pulpit, the beliefs, standards, and laws of marriage as taught by the church. This should be a consistent and continuing ministry at all age levels.
6. Emphasis should be placed on having weddings in church performed by members of the priesthood of the church and after due public notice.

7. Experts in the fields of marriage counseling and skilled medical help should be utilized when indicated, including those available from sources outside the church.
8. Immediate premarital instruction should be specific and given only by experienced physicians and/or marriage counselors.
9. Follow-up, after marriage, should be provided in the total educational program for the purpose of helping newlyweds to make the necessary adjustments between themselves and to the advent of children in the new home. (Adopted October 27, 1955)

II. Maintaining Standards of Marriage

"True marriage is a sacrament, and should not be entered into lightly, hastily, or unworthily" (G.C.R. 972). We therefore advise:

That ministers of the church requested to officiate in marriage cermonies should require that they be given sufficient time by the parties seeking their services to enable them to make such investigation and to give such instruction as these ministers deem necessary in order to insure the maintenance of the sacramental nature of the marriage covenant and of the marriage itself.

That ministers of the church should refuse to officiate at marriage ceremonies where the covenanting parties do not realize the sacramental nature of the covenant, or do not feel deeply their spiritual obligation to abide by its sacrificial demands as well as to enjoy its happy rewards (G.C.R. 972).

That ministers of the church requested to officiate in marriage ceremonies where either or both of the principals are divorced should inquire as to the grounds for the divorce and should satisfy themselves that these grounds are within the areas recognized by the church as permitting remarriage.

Many marriage problems requiring the interpretation of the law of the church should be resolved in harmony with basic policies and by the administrative officers most directly concerned. These church officers are likely to be apprised of the attending circumstances, and to have access to information not readily available at headquarters. Appeals for rulings by persons contemplating marriage will not be acted upon by the First Presidency until the local administrative officer has been respected in his place and a copy of his ruling is available. (Adopted December 18, 1958)

III. Ministry in Marital Difficulties.

1. The primary objective of church ministry in homes having marital difficulties is to bring to bear sound spiritual insights and such spiritual power as will strengthen the marriage ties and thus save the home. The approach therefore is that of a healing ministry rather than that which is inquisitorial or punitive in nature.

2. Inasmuch as husband and wife are "one" in a unique sense, the difficulties that arise between them are frequently more intense and have more far-reaching consequences than difficulties which arise between members not married to each other and whose circumstances do not require the intimate hour-to-hour and day-to-day relationships involved in marriage. Because of this, the responsibility for ministry in homes having marital difficulties should be recognized and accepted by those ministers most fully qualified. Priesthood whose specific duty is in the field of home ministry should be encouraged to prepare for this type of counseling.

3. Desirable qualifications for this ministry include spiritual maturity, sound judgment, genuine personal interest in those having difficulties, and such proficiency in counseling as may be developed through study, experience, and spiritual preparation. This type of ministry requires the very highest and best in wisdom, patience, humility, sympathy, and understanding. In a specific case, personal interest in the counselee and the confidence which this engenders may be determining factors in the selection of one to render the ministry, whether such selection be on the initiative of the parties involved or by pastoral assignment.

4. The one assigned for ministry should in all cases recognize his limitations, and where there is an indicated need for services which he is not prepared to give, he should encourage the parties involved to enlist the services of those especially qualified in the area of need. The ideal situation for ministry is one in which personal interest, priesthood responsibility, and appropriate professional competence are combined in the one person.

5. Even though marital difficulties may be resolved for the time being, they are likely to recur unless the marital situation is constantly strengthened by competent guidance and participation in the full life of the church through consistent church attendance, personal and family worship, mutual participation in Christian service, and similar activities.

6. The pastor or other officer administratively concerned should keep free from involvement in the intimate details of the difficulty except where the situation requires that he shall give the needed counsel. Nevertheless, he should keep in sufficiently close touch with the situation to insure that the maximum facilities of

the church are being made available.

7. Ministers should never recommend or suggest divorce.
8. Knowledge of the healing ministry available for those experiencing marital difficulties should be disseminated throughout the church and those having such difficulties should be encouraged and helped to seek this ministry on their own initiative or, if necessary, at the suggestion of their pastor. (Adopted June 9, 1960)

IV. Leaving Companions for the Sake of Adultery

The law is specific that the one who has left his companion for the sake of adultery shall be cast out (D. and C. 42:20).

It is therefore required that in all cases where it is clearly evident that a married person has forsaken his or her companion for the sake of adultery, and has entered into the marriage relationship with the person for whom he or she forsook his or her companion, the church should inflict on him or her the penalty of expulsion; and that when it is clearly evident that a member of the church has knowingly married a person who left his or her companion in order to enter into this marriage, thereby marrying one who has left his or her companion for the sake of adultery, then the church shall inflict on this member the penalty of expulsion. (Adopted September 20, 1946)

V. Interlocutory Decree of Divorce

In some jurisdictions an interlocutory decree of divorce is granted after the matter is heard by the court, which provides that the divorce does not become final until the end of a specified time.

During this waiting period neither party to the marriage covenant is legally free to remarry. Inasmuch as they are still married persons, both should govern themselves accordingly in their individual relations with other persons of the opposite sex.

The couple and the ministers of the church are urged to regard this waiting period as an opportunity for further efforts toward reconciliation. (Adopted March 18, 1965)

VI. Abortions

Abortions willfully induced for any cause other than that of protecting the life and health of the mother are sinful. Members of the priesthood should labor and counsel against abortions in all situations except where competent medical authority has recommended abortion as a means of protecting the life and health of the mother. (Adopted April 24, 1958)

VII. Adultery and Fornication Defined

When two unmarried persons indulge voluntarily in sexual intercourse, in our administrative and judicial procedure the offense shall be construed as fornication.

When two persons, both or either of whom is married (but not each to the other), are guilty of voluntary sexual intercourse, in our judicial and administrative procedure the offense shall be construed as adultery, with the following reservation: if one of the offenders is unmarried, and it shall be clearly in evidence that this unmarried person was deceived into believing the other offender to be unmarried, said unmarried person shall be held guilty of fornication. (Adopted July 19, 1946)

VIII. Unmarried Parents

Fornication is a sin. When the sin is known, those guilty should be labored with kindly and privately. If they will not repent, charges may be preferred against them in the church courts. But the entire approach, including any court action, should be directed toward repentance and reformation.

There is no requirement for a written statement of confession and repentance before forgiveness can be expressed. Unless the circumstances are such that the facts have caused public concern, a public statement normally is not wise.

When fornication results in a pregnancy and the question of the wisdom of marriage is raised, the following facts should be kept in mind:

Christian marriage is intended as a life partnership based on mutual affection and respect and on the fundamental Christian character of the parties. If such a basis for marriage exists, marriage is generally strongly advisable. But if no such basis exists, marriage should not be advised just because of the pregnancy.

The welfare of the child of the parties should be given major consideration in light of the specific circumstances. This consideration should include such matters as the legitimacy of the child, its financial support, and its prospective home situation after birth.

An equally major concern is the welfare of the mother. This includes the financial cost of the pregnancy and the protection of her future as far as possible. She should not be so concerned about covering up her predicament that she overlooks the future or puts in jeopardy the welfare of her child. For her to be married into an unwholesome situation may eventuate in more sorrow and damage for her and for her child than if she remained unmarried. Despite the importance of privacy, the emphasis in ministry should be on doing what is sound and just and not an attempt to cover up what has happened.

Where the opportunity of ministry is available, each of the parties should be advised and helped to accept willingly the measure of responsibility which the total situation indicates.

In giving such counsel as is herein discussed, all necessary consultation should be had with approved social agencies. Careful attention should also be paid to the legal pro- cedures involved; e.g., representatives of the church should familiarize themselves with laws concerning adoptions and should advise against any procedures which seek to circumvent those laws. (Adopted April 24, 1958)

APPENDIX C

STATEMENTS BY THE FIRST PRESIDENCY
RE MARRIAGE AND FAMILY LIFE

I. Summary of discussion with High Priests Quorum by President Frederick M. Smith, April 7, 1936

"We must begin one hundred years before the divorce to solve the marriage problem," declared President Frederick M. Smith before the Quorum of High Priests Tuesday morning. The quorum was in session in the choir room at its regular ten o'clock hour. The question of marriage standards was the subject of the hour.

In making his approach to the subject President Smith called attention to the vast difference in the standards of marriage that were in existence in the time of Christ, when most of our scriptural bases were established, and the present status. From the position in which the wife was a mere chattel of the simplest sort to one in which she enjoys a social position equal to that of her husband marks the progress in the social aspect of marriage.

Not only in the address of President Smith but in the discussion by the various members of the quorum was it quite evident that the general feeling was one of a sympathetic interest in those involved in marital difficulties. Those in trouble were to be assisted in every way possible and the first consideration was that of saving as much of the human wreckage as possible.

In emphasizing his point President Smith said, "Personally and officially I am inclined to become much more lenient in regard to the situation than I was in the early days of my experience in the Presidency."

The discussion brought out many questions of which the following are quite typical. "Can any positive law be laid down that will fit all cases as pertains to the right to remarry after having been divorced?" "Are there more grounds for divorce which can be recognized than the one of adultery?" "How much must the welfare of the children of the home be recognized in determining the advisability of divorce or the right to remarry?" "Do divorced church members who are remarried have a right to any protection from the church if their case has been properly investigated and said to have sufficient merit to make remarriage permissible?"

In making a general reply to these questions the speaker stated that all marriages should be deliberately formed and religiously celebrated. He called attention to the statement also that in the marriage covenant both parties pledged not only to "keep themselves from all others" but also to keep themselves "for each other."

While it was admitted that no positive set of regulations could be set down which would equitably meet the needs of all cases it was thought that a clearer understanding of procedure would be possible if a general statement could be formulated. This the quorum may attempt to do before final adjournment.

"There must be an influence thrown around the children of the home to educate them to think in terms of building permanent homes, homes that are admittedly holy, and to move forward with this in mind in the selection of their companions." This statement from the President's address sums up much of the task set out for the church in the beginning of our educational campaign in an attempt to solve the problem.—"President Smith Discusses Marriage Problems," *Daily Herald*, April 8, 1936, pp. 57, 62.

II. From President Frederick M. Smith's Address to the World Conference, April 3, 1938

In the following comments on the church and youth, I am repeating largely what I said some years ago in addressing this body. Our youth present a whole series of problems. In saying this I am not disposed to put the blame wholly upon the youth, for I feel we should frankly face the fact that the blame is largely ours. Our youth are about what we make them. They are what they are because of the forces and the conditions and the environments in which we have compelled them to move and to be. And we in the same spirit of frankness ask what we are doing to meet the problems they present? What are we doing to keep our youth constantly interested in church activities? Jazz and youth's response to it are but the outcrop of forces which lie beneath, and forces with which we must reckon. The problem of controlling those forces lies close to that of creating a proper recreation for our youth, but our treatment must be positive, not negative, and this demands something more than a mere negative attitude towards commercialized recreation.

And closely allied to the problems of youth I have mentioned is the question of marriage and procreation, of divorce and remarriage, etc., for these affect the fundamental question of family and family life, and thus involve large social questions. The forces without our own circles, everywhere making themselves felt, and from the effects of which we have not escaped, which tend towards destroying the sanctity of the marriage covenant, suggests the necessity of the church attempting solution of this group of problems in the interests of a safer and more stable social growth. Always must we stand for and emphasize that which will reestablish and maintain among our people the sanctity of marriage, and the necessity of surrounding the forming of new family relations with such religious atmosphere and social importance as will cause our youth to look upon marriage as a deeply sacred institution which must be approached with solemnity and a sense of responsibility to Divinity. To so impress our youth with the sanctity of the home will go far towards solving many of the problems of youth, and also in the solution of the problems of divorce. For when there is proper preparation for marriage, when companionships are formed with due recognition that steps are being taken which will deeply affect the lives of the contracting parties as well as others, for life, hasty marriages will be lessened, and the causes for and of divorce concomitantly checked.

And this suggests that the problem is not to be solved by legislative action alone. Create within our people, old and young, the right attitude towards family life, and we will have no need to legislate on these problems. The approach, then, to the problems of marriage and divorce, bound up as they are with the larger social question of the social meaning of family, presents a task in education of our youth in the social as well as individual importance of selecting mates. We have not been wisely active in such educational endeavors. It is not only education which is needed there, but education strongly impregnated with religion and sense of responsibility to God. To undertake this properly will be to attempt to create within our youth and those forming homes, a sense of responsibility to others as well as self, and even to future generations as well as to the present, an enlargement or expansion of the real spirit of altruism which must saturate any society which we on the basis of our religion shall attempt to form.—*Daily Herald*, April 5, 1938, p. 56.

III. From the Report of the First Presidency to the 1958 World Conference

We have reason to deplore the extent to which the current standards in relation to divorce and remarriage are followed by our people. We have been seeking to make constructive approaches to this problem, which will be brought before the Conference by a resolution proposed from the San Francisco Bay District. But it should be recognized that no negative attack will be widely successful; no barriers and denunciations will be of significant creative worth. The solution of the problems in this area, as of all our major problems, lies in the total ministry of the church and especially in our ministry to our children and young people. It is on this foundation that we must give our specific ministries in crucial situations.—*General Conference Bulletin*, 1958, p. 70.

IV. From the Address by President W. Wallace Smith to the 1960 World Conference

It is of the utmost importance that our young people shall be involved in the whole work of the church. Recreation and special service projects are desirable but are not enough in themselves. Effective ministry to the youth involves their participation in the total program of the church. We strongly urge that our young people be invited to be faithful in attendance at preaching services, in the church school and League meetings, at the other services of worship, and most particularly that they share in the ordinances of the gospel. They have a great opportunity in evangelism through their contacts with friends at school and in their social activities. But if this important work is to be successfully carried out among our young people, the basis for it must be laid in wholesome family life. Then, with care, this may be brought to fruition in growing maturity, through courtship and marriage, and in the eventual establishment of Zionic homes by people with Zionic backgrounds.—*General Conference Bulletin*, 1960, p. 78.

V. From the Report of the First Presidency to the 1964 World Conference

The leading officers of the church, both general and local, have long been concerned about strengthening the families of the church through better ministry. In recent months considerable progress has been made in developing visual aids and other materials especially adapted to home ministry. Assignments in this field will be announced at the close of the Conference and put into effect as quickly thereafter as circumstances permit. In the field of home ministry the work of members of the Bishopric and of their associates of the Aaronic priesthood is of great importance. Our people cannot be free so long as they are in debt, and those who have to do with shaping the ways of thought and action of the Saints in their personal affairs, members of both priesthoods, should keep in mind that there is no true freedom for persons who are ignorant, or ridden by evil habit, or the prey of passing whims. If we would become a great people, we must first of all become a happily self-disciplined people who willingly make the sacrifices which are incident to growth and power in ministry.—*World Conference Bulletin*, 1964, p. 283.